GCSE | 9-1

geography

EDEXCEL B

Exam Practice

Series editor
Bob Digby   **Nicholas Rowles**

OXFORD
UNIVERSITY PRESS

OXFORD

UNIVERSITY PRESS

Great Clarendon Street, Oxford, OX2 6DP, United Kingdom

Oxford University Press is a department of the University of Oxford. It furthers the University's objective of excellence in research, scholarship, and education by publishing worldwide. Oxford is a registered trade mark of Oxford University Press in the UK and in certain other countries

© Oxford University Press 2019

Series editor: Bob Digby

Authors: Bob Digby and Nicholas Rowles

British Library Cataloguing in Publication Data
Data available

ISBN 978-019-843617-1

10 9 8 7 6 5 4 3 2 1

Paper used in the production of this book is a natural, recyclable product made from wood grown in sustainable forests. The manufacturing process conforms to the environmental regulations of the country of origin.

Printed in Great Britain by Bell and Bain Ltd., Glasgow

Acknowledgements

The publisher and authors would like to thank the following for permission to use photographs and other copyright material:

Cover: Revenant/Shutterstock; **p15:** RomeoFox/Alamy Stock Photo; **p70:** GavinD/iStockphoto; **p71:** Mika Schick/Alamy Stock Photo; **p79:** The Photolibrary Wales/Alamy Stock Photo; **p80:** Andrew Stacey/www.stacey.peak-media.co.uk; **p86:** Chris Green/Shutterstock; **p116:** NurPhoto/Getty Images; **p122:** Peeter Viisimaa/Getty Images; **p126:** Steve Outram/Alamy Stock Photo; **p130:** geogphotos/Alamy Stock Photo; **p132(tl):** Dave Bagnall/Alamy Stock Photo; **p132(tr):** DigitalVues/Alamy Stock Photo; **p132(bl):** Zoonar GmbH/Alamy Stock Photo; **p132(br):** Theo Moye/Alamy Stock Photo; **p133:** Nick Rowles; **p136:** Phil Wills/Alamy Stock Photo; **p159(tl):** Marques/Shutterstock; **p159(tm):** AlxYago/Shutterstock; **p159(tr):** Volodymyr Burdiak/Shutterstock; **p159(bl):** Wolfgang Kaehler/Getty Images; **p159(br):** Francesco Dazzi/Shutterstock; **p167:** jeffdalt/iStockphoto; **p169:** CC BY 3.0/Molinario, Giuseppe & C Hansen, M & V Potapov, P & Tyukavina, Alexandra & Stehman, Stephen & Barker, B & Humber, M. (2017). Quantification of land cover and land use within the rural complex of the Democratic Republic of Congo. Environmental Research Letters. 12. 104001. 10.1088/1748-9326/aa8680; **p173:** Rebecca Blackwell/AP/Shutterstock; **p174:** Jake Lyell/Alamy Stock Photo; **p175:** Georg Gerster/Panos.

Artwork by Aptara Inc., Kamae Design, Lovell Johns, Barking Dog Art, and Q2A Media Services Inc.

Every effort has been made to contact copyright holders of material reproduced in this book. Any omissions will be rectified in subsequent printings if notice is given to the publisher.

Guided answers and mark schemes are available on the Oxford Secondary Geography website: **www.oxfordsecondary.co.uk/geography-answers**

Please note: The Practice Paper exam-style questions and mark schemes have not been written or approved by Edexcel. The answers and commentaries provided represent one interpretation only and other solutions may be appropriate.

Introduction

How to be successful in your exams

If you want to be successful in your exams, then you need to know how you will be examined, what kinds of questions you will come up against in the exam, how to use what you know, and what you will get marks for. That's where this book can help.

How to use this book

This book contains the following features to help you prepare for exams for the Edexcel B GCSE 9–1 Geography specification. It is written to work alongside two other OUP publications to support your learning:

- *GCSE 9–1 Geography Edexcel B Student Book*
- *GCSE 9–1 Geography Edexcel B Revision Guide*.

An introduction (pages 4–12)

This section contains details about:

- the exam papers you'll be taking, and what you need to revise for each exam paper
- how exam papers are marked, and how to aim for the highest grades.

On your marks (pages 13–63)

This section contains guidance about how to answer questions about specific topics using extended writing for 4, 6, 8, and 12 marks in Papers 1–3. There is space for you to write and assess exam answers so you learn how to write good quality answers.

Exam papers (pages 64–176)

This section contains two sets of exam papers. These are written to match the style of those you'll meet in the Edexcel GCSE B Geography exam. Each set contains:

- Exam Papers 1 and 2 which assess your knowledge and understanding of the course, together with fieldwork in Paper 2. You'll have two days fieldwork during the course to use in answering this part of the exam – one day physical geography and one human.
- Exam Paper 3 which assesses a decision-making exercise (usually called a DME). This assesses your knowledge, understanding and skills in interpreting an unseen Resource Booklet. During the exam, you'll use the booklet to understand the geographical issues on which it is based, and your geographical skills in making sense of it.

Each exam paper has space for answers, like a real exam. There is an online mark scheme (for your teacher to use).

Edexcel's GCSE Geography specification consists of three components. Each component contains topics. Each component is assessed by an exam paper (Papers 1, 2 and 3) with sections for different topics, as on the next page:

Component 1 Global geographical issues

This is assessed by Paper 1 in the exam. There are three sections, each on different topics. All questions are compulsory.

- **Section A**: Topic 1 *Hazardous Earth*, with questions on the *Global climate system*, *Climate change*, *Extreme weather* (e.g. tropical cyclones) and *Tectonic hazards*.
- **Section B**: Topic 2 *Development dynamics*, with questions on *Global development*, and a case study of one of the world's emerging countries.
- **Section C**: Topic 3 *Challenges of an urbanising world*, with questions on *Rapid urbanisation* and *Global urban trends*, and a case study of one of the world's megacities in either a developing or an emerging country.

In addition, questions will assess your geographical skills (e.g. interpreting statistics, maps, diagrams) within each topic.

Memory jogger for Paper 1!

- My case study of an emerging country was of _____

- My case study of a developing or an emerging country was of _____, which is a developing/ emerging country (*delete one*).

Component 2 UK Geographical Issues

This is assessed by Paper 2 in the exam. There are four sections, each on a different topic, with a choice of fieldwork questions.

- **Section A** includes Topic 4 *The UK's evolving physical landscape* with questions on the UK's physical landscape, *Coastal change and conflict*, and *River processes and pressures*.
- **Section B** includes Topic 5 *The UK's evolving human landscape* with questions on the *UK's changing population* and a case study of one major UK city.
- **Sections C1 and C2** includes Topic 6 *Geographical investigations* with questions on fieldwork in Section C1 on **either** *Coastal change and conflict* **or** *River processes and pressures*, and in Section C2 on **either** *Dynamic urban areas* or *Changing rural areas*.

Like Paper 1, questions will assess your skills within each topic.

Memory jogger for Paper 2!

- My case study of a major UK city was of _____

- My physical fieldwork was on rivers/coasts (*delete one*) and we collected data on _____ at _____. (*name of place*)

- My human fieldwork was on cities/rural areas (*delete one*) and we collected data on _____ at _____. (*name of place*)

Component 3 Making geographical decisions

This is assessed by Paper 3 in the examination. It consists of an unseen Resource Booklet with the following sections:

- **Section A**: Topic 7 *People and the biosphere*
- **Section B**: Topic 8 *Forests under threat*
- **Section C**: Topic 9 *Consuming energy resources*
- **Section D**: A geographical decision-making question.

All three exam papers are quite different from each other.

Format of Paper 1

- **Time**: 1 hour 30 minutes.
- **Worth**: 94 marks in total – 90 marks on the three topics you've learned, and another 4 for spelling, punctuation, grammar and use of specialist geographical terminology (SPaG) which is assessed on one 8-mark question in Section B.
- **Counts for**: 37.5% of your final grade.
- **Number of sections**: three, assessing the topics described in Component 1 on page 5.

You must answer all questions as follows:

- **Section A**: *Hazardous Earth* – questions on the *Global climate system*, *Climate change*, *Extreme weather* (e.g. tropical cyclones) and *Tectonic hazards*. This section has 30 marks.
- **Section B**: *Development dynamics* – questions on *Global development*, and a case study of **one** of the world's emerging countries. This section has 30 marks.
- **Section C**: *Challenges of an urbanising world* – questions on *Rapid urbanisation* and *Global urban trends*, and a case study of one of the world's megacities in **either** a developing **or** an emerging country. This section has 30 marks.

One question in Paper 1 carries 4 marks for SPaG.

Any resources that you need to answer the questions are included – there is no separate Resource Booklet.

Format of Paper 2

- **Time**: 1 hour 30 minutes.
- **Worth**: 94 marks in total – 90 marks on topics you've learned, and another 4 for SPaG, which is assessed on one question in Section A.
- **Counts for**: 37.5% of your final grade.
- **Number of sections**: four, assessing the topics described in Component 2 on page 5.

You must answer:

- **all** parts of **Section A**: *The UK's evolving physical landscape* – questions on the UK's physical landscape, *Coastal change and conflict*, and *River processes and pressures*. This section has 27 marks plus 4 for SPaG.
- **all** parts of **Section B**: *The UK's evolving human landscape* – questions on the *UK's changing population* and a case study of one major UK city. This section has 27 marks.
- **two** questions on fieldwork in **Section C**. One must be from Section C1 on **either** *Coastal change and conflict* **or** *River processes and pressures*, and the second from Section C2 on **either** *Dynamic urban areas* or *Changing rural areas*. Each of these has 18 marks.

Any resources you need to answer the questions are included – there is no separate Resource Booklet.

Format of Paper 3

- **Time**: 1 hour 30 minutes.
- **Worth**: 64 marks in total – 60 for geographical questions, and 4 marks for SPaG which are assessed in the final question in Section D.
- **Counts for**: 25% of your final grade.
- **Number of sections**: four

You must answer all questions as follows:

- **Section A**: questions on *People and the biosphere*. This section has 8 marks.
- **Section B**: questions on *Forests under threat*. This section has 7 marks.
- **Section C**: questions on *Consuming energy resources*. This section has 33 marks.
- **Section D**: a geographical decision-making question. This question carries 12 marks plus 4 for SPaG.

Paper 3 has a separate Resource Booklet.

Question style

The first questions in each section are short and worth between 1 and 4 marks.

- These include a mix of multiple-choice, short answers, or calculations.
- There are resource materials (data, photos, cartoons, etc.) on which you'll be asked questions. These could include statistical skills, so remember you can use a calculator in each exam.
- You'll be expected to know what these resources are getting at from what you've learned.
- Detailed case study knowledge is only needed for the case studies in Papers 1 and 2 – though you can get marks for using examples.

All these questions are **point marked**.

Later questions in each section require extended writing, and are worth 8 marks. Paper 3 also contains one question of 12 marks. You need to have learned examples and case studies to answer these questions. Answers like this are marked using **levels** – from Level 1 (lowest) to Level 3 (highest) – see page 10. These questions are likely to be on those parts where you have been taught examples (e.g. on Paper 1 a tectonic hazard, a tropical cyclone event, or emerging country).

One 8-mark question on each paper is also assessed for SPaG for 4 marks – making it worth 12 marks total.

Answering the questions

Answering questions properly is the key to success. When you first read an exam question, check out the **command word** – that is, the word that the examiner uses to tell you what to do. Figure 1 gives you the command words you can expect, and the number of marks you can expect for each command word.

Command word	Typical no. of marks	What the command word means	Example of a question
Identify/State/ Name	1	Find (e.g. on a photo), or give a simple word or statement	Identify the landform shown in the photo *or* Name City *a* on map 2.
Define	1	Give a clear meaning	Define the term 'fertility rate'.
Calculate	1 or 2	Work out	Calculate the mean depth of the river shown in Figure *W*.
Label	1 or 2	Print the name of, or write, on a map or diagram	Label the two features A and B of the cliff in Figure *X*.
Draw	2 or 3	As in sketch or drawing a line	Draw a line to complete the graph in Figure *Y*.
Compare	3	Identify similarities or differences	*(referring to a graph)* Compare the rate of population growth in city *b* with city *c*.
Describe	2 or 3	Say what something is like; identify trends (e.g. on a graph)	Describe the features on the photo shown in Figure *Z*.
Explain	2, 3 or 4	Give reasons why something happens	Explain the rapid growth of one named megacity you have studied.
Suggest	2, 3 or 4	In an unfamiliar situation (e.g. a photo or graph), explain how or why something might occur, giving a reason.	Suggest reasons for the increase shown in the graph.
Assess	8	Weigh up which is most/least important	Assess the need for coastal management along a stretch of coast you have studied.
Evaluate	8	Make judgements about which is most or least effective	Evaluate the methods used in collecting data in your fieldwork.
Justify	12	Give reasons why you support a particular decision or opinion	*(in Paper 3, last question)* Justify the reasons for your choice.

Figure 1 *Meaning of command words, marks available and examples*

Examiners have clear guidance about how to mark. They must mark fairly, so that the first candidate's exam paper in a pile is marked in exactly the same way as the last. You will be rewarded for what you know and can do; you won't lose marks for what you leave out. If your answer matches the best qualities in the mark scheme then you'll get full marks.

Questions that carry between 1 and 4 marks are **point marked**, and those carrying 8 marks or more are **level marked**. Be clear about what this means.

Understanding Assessment Objectives

Assessment Objectives (called AOs) are the things that examiners look for in marking your answers. There are four in GCSE Geography:

- AO1 – Knowledge recall
- AO2 – Understanding of concepts, places and environments
- AO3 – Applying ideas to situations, and making informed judgements
- AO4 – Geographical skills, which includes fieldwork, stats and maths skills

Command word	Assessment Objective	Example of a question assessing this AO
Identify/State/ Name	AO1	Identify the landform shown in the photo *or* Name City *a* on Map 2.
Define	AO1	Define the term 'fertility rate'.
Calculate	AO4	Calculate the mean depth of the river shown in Figure *W*.
Label	AO1	Label features A and B of the cliff in Figure *X*.
Draw	AO4	Draw a line to complete the graph in Figure *Y*.
Compare	AO3	Compare the rate of population growth in city *b* with city *c*.
Describe	AO1 & 2	Describe the features of a river meander.
Explain	AO1 & 2	Explain the rapid growth of one megacity you have studied.
Suggest	AO3	Suggest reasons for the increase shown in the graph.
Assess (8 marks)	Paper 1: AO2 and AO3 (4 marks each) *or* Paper 2: AO3 and AO4 (4 marks each)	*(Paper 1)* Assess the impacts of a named tropical cyclone. *(Paper 2)* Assess the likely impact of the storm shown in Figure *Z*.
Evaluate (8 marks)	Paper 1: AO2 and AO3 (4 marks each) *or* Paper 2: AO3 and AO4 (4 marks each)	*(Paper 1)* Evaluate whether tectonic hazards have greater impacts on developed than on developing countries. *(Paper 2)* Evaluate the methods used in collecting data in your fieldwork.
Justify (12 marks)	AO2, AO3 and AO4 (4 marks each)	*(in Paper 3, last question)* Justify the reasons for your choice.

Figure 2 *Examples of the command words used for each AO and typical questions. 'Assess', 'Evaluate' and 'Justify' are the most challenging.*

Understanding the most demanding questions

The last three command words in Figure 2 are the most demanding. They

- assess AO3
- form the extended written questions
- carry highest marks.

Figure 2 shows that questions often combine marks for AO3 with marks for other AOs. Examples where AO3 is used with AO2 include:

- *Assess the impacts of a named tropical cyclone (8 marks).* This involves you knowing and understanding impacts of tropical cyclones (that's AO2 – understanding) for 4 marks and then assessing how serious each impact is (so that's AO3 – application) for another 4.

Sometimes AO3 is used with AO4. Examples include:

- *Evaluate the methods used in collecting data in your fieldwork (8 marks).* This involves you using your experience of fieldwork skills (AO4) for 4 marks and then making a judgement about how well or how accurately these methods worked (so that's AO3 – application) for another 4.

In Paper 3, three AOs are assessed in the final 12-mark question:

- *Justify the reasons for your choice (8 marks).* This involves using data in the Resource Booklet (AO4) for 4 marks, using what you have learned in the course (AO2) for another 4, and then how you use these to make a judgement about which is the best option (that's AO3 – application) for a further 4 marks.

Note in each case that to get full marks, you must address each AO.

Level-marked questions

Longer questions worth 8 or 12 marks are marked using levelled mark schemes. Examiners mark answers based on these. Figure 4 shows an 8-mark scheme.

- There are three levels; Level 1 is the lowest and Level 3 the highest.
- Figure 3 is a detailed summary of what examiners look for.
- Note that it is not so much the number of points you make that matter, but the ways in which these are explained and extended.

Tip

You can find more detailed guidance on answering 8- and 12-mark questions in the 'On your marks' pages 22–63.

		0	No acceptable response.
1	1–3		• Limited or no explanation. • One or two points are simply described but not developed. • Most of the answer lacks detail or named examples. • Places are poorly located (e.g. 'in Africa'). • Few geographical terms or phrases. • Makes no judgement when asked to 'assess' or 'evaluate'.
2	4–6		• Some fairly clear explanation. • Two or three points are explained briefly with some development. • Examples are used, but vary in detail; places (e.g. countries) and impacts are named. • Writes clearly, using some geographical terms. • Makes some judgement when asked to 'assess' or 'evaluate'.
3	7–8		• Explains very clearly. • Makes detailed points, using extended explanations to develop the answer. • Detailed examples are used; specific places and impacts are named. • Well written, with full use of geographical terms. • Makes detailed judgements based on evidence when asked to 'assess' or 'evaluate'.

Figure 3 Level marking – a summary of what examiners look for

Using the command word 'Assess'

When they mark, examiners do not mark points, but instead read the answer as a whole, and judge it against the qualities shown in Figure 4 – a detailed level-based mark scheme for all 8-mark questions which assess AO2 and AO3. For 8 marks you need about three extended and exemplified points. Level 3 is reserved for candidates who 'assess' as the command word tells them to do.

Level	Marks	Descriptor
	0	No acceptable response.
1	1–3	• Limited understanding of concepts and links between places, environments and processes. (AO2) • Some application and understanding, though links may be flawed. (AO3) • An imbalanced or incomplete argument showing little understanding. Judgements supported by limited evidence. (AO3)
2	4–6	• Some understanding of concepts and links between places, environments and processes. (AO2) • Generally applies understanding to deconstruct information and provide some logical links between concepts. (AO2) • An imbalanced argument – mostly coherent explanations, leading to generalised judgements supported by some evidence. (AO3)
3	7–8	• Accurate understanding of concepts and links between places, environments and processes. (AO2) • Applies understanding to deconstruct information and provide logical links between concepts. (AO3) • A balanced, well-developed argument with coherent relevant explanations, leading to judgements supported by evidence. (AO3)

Figure 4 A mark scheme using levels of response

How to 'assess' and produce a Level 3 answer

Figure 5 shows a Level 3 answer to the question *'Assess the economic effects of a named tropical storm.'* *(8 marks).* It is worth the full 8 marks.

The storm is named. Always do this – you could limit yourself to Level 1 or 2 if you don't. Notice the phrase *'most serious'* – it is evidence the candidate is assessing this impact

Credit is given for the detailed explanation of the economic effects of a storm – *'damaged buildings'*, *'costing insurance companies and governments millions'*. This makes the answer Level 3 because of the detail. The candidate is also assessing the storm as the 'worst known'.

'In Cyclone Aila which affected Bangladesh in 2009 the economic effects were enormous, and were most serious among the poor. The cyclone brought some of the worst known stormy winds and floods. This damaged buildings, which cost insurance companies and governments millions. More storms also caused erosion of flood defences, which flooded villages and farmland costing huge amounts to replace and repair, and destroyed crops. For many farmers and families, this meant loss of homes and crops, making their poverty worse and forcing some to leave the land and move to Dhaka, the capital, for work.'

'Erosion of flood defences' is an economic impact. The phrase *'costing huge amounts'* is a judgement of its seriousness, making this answer Level 3, and showing that the candidate is assessing.

'loss of homes and crops' is evidence of another economic impact. The candidate assesses the seriousness of loss of crops – it makes poverty worse and forces people to leave the land. This judgement answers the command word 'Assess'.

Figure 5 An example of a Level 3 answer

Always make sure you answer the question that is set!

- Good answers are usually focused – without straying off the point.
- Good answers are more likely if you unpick the question, as shown below.

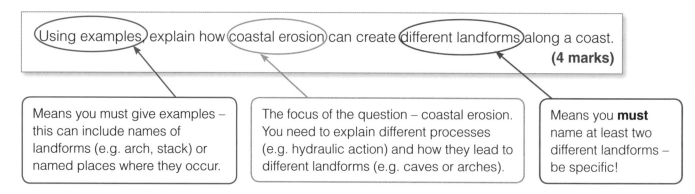

This question is about explaining processes that lead to different landforms such as arches. It's important that you explain why these processes happen – don't just describe. Good explanation takes you to Level 3.

Using case studies

Candidates worry about case studies – how to learn them and write a good answer. The following question requires the use of examples.

> 'Evaluate the success of regeneration in one named UK city.' **(8 marks)**

This question could be answered using the example of east London (see student book sections 5.10–5.15). But use other examples if you wish.

A good way to plan case studies is to use a spider diagram like the one below.

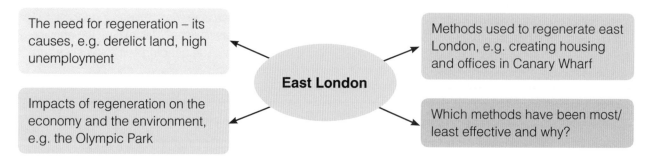

Once you have drawn this diagram, build up detailed notes, e.g.

'*The need for regeneration*' – draw two 'legs' from this box to explain economic causes (e.g. lack of jobs) and environmental (e.g. derelict land).

- '*Methods used to regenerate east London, e.g. creating housing and offices*' – draw three 'legs' to explain methods used to provide housing for people, build the economy, and improve the environment.
- '*Impacts of regeneration on the economy and the environment*' – you could sub-divide these too, into economic, social and environmental impacts.
- Finally, you could draw two 'legs' to show which methods have been effective and which have not.

On your marks

Maximising marks on shorter questions

- **In this section you'll learn how to maximise marks on questions carrying between 1 and 4 marks.**

Getting the answer right

Answering questions properly is the key to success. When you read an exam question, check two things:

- the **command word** – this is what the examiner wants you to do (see page 8)
- the **number of marks** – this tells you how many points to make.

Questions carrying up to 4 marks are point marked – that means you get a mark for every correct point you make.

Understanding point marking

Look at this question:

> Rainforests are ecosystems. State **one** way in which people can protect ecosystems. **(1 mark)**

Because there is one mark for this question, you have to name one way of protecting ecosystems, for example:

- *set up a national park* or
- *make it illegal to carry out logging.*

You get one mark for a correct answer. The mark scheme tells examiners which points they can mark as correct.

Extending an answer – 'Describe'

Success on longer questions with more marks means knowing how to turn 1 mark into 2, or 2 into 3. To achieve this, you need to **develop** answers.

Look at this question:

> Rainforests are ecosystems. Describe **one** way in which humans can protect ecosystems. **(2 marks)**

This time, it is not enough to name one way of protecting an ecosystem. To earn 2 marks, you must do one of the following:

- **extend the point** by describing in more detail, e.g. *make it illegal to carry out logging where forest habitats are protected for animals*
- **give an example** of what you are describing, e.g. *make it illegal to carry out logging, for example, like the rainforests in large areas of Brazil*
- **give a reason** why something occurs, e.g. *make it illegal to carry out logging because that is the biggest danger to rainforest ecosystems.*

Extending an answer – 'Explain'

Now consider this question:

> Explain one possible economic impact of climate change. **(2 marks)**

This question asks you to 'explain' (give reasons for) the impacts.

- That means you shouldn't just state what the impact is but **why** it occurs.
- It's the explanation that earns marks.
- In the following examples, a tick is used to show where a mark is earned. Look at the comments in the side panels.

> Rising sea level might mean farmland near the coast gets flooded. ✔

However:

> Rising sea level might mean farmland near the coast gets flooded ✔ **so that** farmers lose their crops. ✔

Other examples of extended answers include:

> Sea level change might mean farmland near the coast gets flooded ✔ **and farmers would lose crops e.g. rice.** ✔

> Sea level change might mean farmers near the coast might lose rice crops ✔ if saltwater flooded the fields **as rice is a freshwater plant.** ✔

> This is an impact – but it is only worth 1 mark as it simply says one thing.

> This is worth 2 marks.
> - The explanation has been **extended** to earn the second mark.
> - The connecting phrase '**so that**' is really useful in getting higher marks!
> - Other useful connecting phrases include '**therefore**', or '**which leads to**'.

> This is an economic impact which has been extended with an **example**, so it gains a second mark.

> This is an example of an answer which has been **explained** – it gives a reason why crops are lost.

Chains of reasoning

In the following example you have to think of four points that run in a sequence, to give a full explanation of a process of how one thing leads to another.

> Explain how volcanoes may form along a constructive plate margin. **(4 marks)**

Below is an example of a **chain of reasoning** – an explanation of a process, e.g. *'x happens which leads to y, and then on to z'.* (Note that this candidate has gone further than needed by making six points.)

> As the plates pull apart (1), a plume of magma rises to the surface to fill the gap (2). At constructive plate margins this is often basaltic lava which flows easily away from the boundary before it solidifies (3). More lava creates another layer on top of the first layer (4). This continues, building up the volcano (5) until it's large with shallow sides (6).

Over to you

Use a chain of reasoning to explain:

- a physical process (e.g. how cliffs become undercut, or how ox-bow lakes form)
- a human process (e.g. how the multiplier effect works).

On your marks

Nailing the 4-mark questions

- **In this section you'll learn how to maximise marks on 4-mark questions.**

Study Figure 1. It shows a house damaged by tropical cyclone Haiyan in a rural area of the Philippines in 2013.

Figure 1

Question

Using Figure 1 and your own knowledge, explain why tropical cyclones have such a big impact in countries like the Philippines.

(4 marks)

Five steps to success!

The following five steps are used in this chapter to help you get the best marks.

1 **Plan your answer** – decide what to include and how to structure your answer.

2 **Write your answer** – use the answer spaces to complete your answer.

3 **Mark your answer** – use the mark scheme to self- or peer-mark your answer. You can also use this to assess sample answers in step 4 below.

4 **Sample answers** – sample answers are given to show you how to maximise marks for a question.

5 **Marked sample answers** – these are the same answers as for step 4, but are marked and annotated, so that you can compare these with your own.

1 Plan your answer

Before attempting to answer the question, remember to **BUG** it. That means:

✓ **Box** the command word.
✓ **Underline** the following:
  - the theme
  - the focus
  - any evidence required
  - the number of examples needed.
✓ **Glance** back over the question – to make sure you include everything in your answer.

Use the BUG on the next page to plan your own answer.

Nailing the 4-mark questions

Evidence: Support your answer with information from the photo, AND from your own knowledge. You must do both to get 4 marks.

Command word: 'Explain' – give reasons why something happens.

Using Figure 1 and your own knowledge, explain two reasons why tropical cyclones have such a big impact on developing countries like the Philippines. **(4 marks)**

Number of examples: The question asks for two specific reasons about developing countries, so you must offer two, **AND** expand them with more detail.

Theme: This question is linked to the theme of tropical cyclones, assessed in Paper 1, Section A of your exam. The question is compulsory.

Focus: You must consider why the hazard has such an impact, not just describe what you see in the photo.

PEEL your answer

Use PEEL notes to structure your answer. This will help you to communicate your ideas to the examiner in the clearest way. PEEL has four stages:

- **P**oint – Make two points for this question. Use sentences, not bullet points.
- **E**vidence – Include details that you know or which come from the photo to support each point.
- **E**xplain – Give reasons for each point. Use sentence starters such as: 'This is because ...', 'One reason is ...'.
- **L**ink – Link the two points to each other, use PEE sentence starters such as: 'A second way is .....' or 'Secondly ...'. You'll learn more about how to do this on 8-mark questions.

Tip

For all questions using 'Explain' as a command word, you will be marked on the number of points you make; 4 marks means two developed points.

② Write your answer

Using Figure 1 and your own knowledge, explain why tropical cyclones have such a big impact in countries like the Philippines. **(4 marks)**

1. _____

_____

_____

2. _____

_____

_____

③ Mark your answer

1. To help you to identify if the answer includes well-structured points, first highlight the:

- points in red
- explanations in orange
- evidence in blue.

2. Use the mark scheme below to decide what mark to give.

Mark Scheme

The candidate must refer to the photo AND their own knowledge. However, points observed in the photo can be explained using their own knowledge, so two points from the photo are acceptable if reasons clearly come from the candidate's own knowledge.

Accept any of the following points for 1 mark each with development as shown:

- *the photo shows a collapsed house (1), which has probably been caused by weak building regulations that are sometimes found in developing countries (1).*
- *Poor quality housing (1) has not been able to withstand strong winds of a tropical cyclone (1).*

- *People in rural areas, like in the photo, may be very vulnerable (1) because they are isolated (1)/difficult to rescue or help (1).*
- *Building materials, e.g. wood, bamboo (1), show the building was probably cheap to build but weak (1).*
- *Plus any other relevant points on merit.*

④ Sample answers

Read through Sample answers 1 and 2 below.

a) Go through each one using the three colours in section 3 above.
b) Decide how many marks each is worth.

Sample answer 1

1. Tropical cyclones have such a big impact in countries like this because houses like the one in the photo would have collapsed, because of the high winds in a tropical cyclone.

2. Tropical cyclones affect the poor most of all as they have no resilience, because they have no savings to fall back on if they lose their house.

Sample answer 2

1. Wooden shacks like the one in the photo are not strong enough to stand up to strong hurricane winds.

2. People in poor countries often live in houses like this on land which isn't theirs.

Strengths of the answer		
Ways to improve the answer		
Level		Mark	

5 Marked sample answers

Sample answers 1 and 2 are marked below. The following have been highlighted to show how well each answer has structured points:

- points in red
- explanations in orange
- evidence in blue.

Ticks are given where the candidate earns a mark. One tick = 1 mark.

Marked sample answer 1

Evidence – collapsed wooden building in the photo

Explanation – suggests that high winds destroyed it

Point – the poor suffer greatest impact because of lack of resilience

Explanation – the reason is given that the poor have no savings

1. Tropical cyclones have such a big impact in countries like this because houses like the one in the photo would have collapsed, ✓ because of the high winds in a tropical cyclone ✓

2. Tropical cyclones affect the poor most of all as they have no resilience, ✓ because they have no savings to fall back on if they lose their house. ✓

 Examiner feedback

The ticks show where marks have been awarded. The candidate uses the photo to identify features which help to answer the question in the first point, and their own knowledge about the impacts of tropical cyclones on poorer people in the second point. Each point is then extended, so that the answer earns all 4 marks.

Marked sample answer 2

Evidence – specific building materials from the photo

Explanation – gives a reason why houses are not strong

1. Wooden shacks like the one in the photo are not strong enough ✓ to stand up to strong hurricane winds. ✓

2. People in poor countries often live in houses like this on land which isn't theirs.

 Examiner feedback

Again, the ticks show where marks have been awarded. Like the first answer, the candidate refers to the photo to identify features about building materials and then how these cannot resist strong hurricane winds. However, although the candidate gives reasons why poor people are more vulnerable in the second point, it doesn't answer this question. Therefore the answer earns just 2 marks.

Now try this one!

Follow the stages from the previous answer to tackle a different 4-mark question.

Figure 2 shows three indicators of development for three countries.

Country	HDI	Death rate per 1000 population	% population with access to safe water
Japan	0.891	9.51	100
Brazil	0.755	6.58	98
Zimbabwe	0.509	10.13	77

Figure 2

Question

Explain the strengths and limitations of any **one** of the indicators in Figure 2 in seeking to understand a country's level of development.

(4 marks)

1 Plan your answer

Before attempting to answer the question, remember to **BUG** it. On a separate piece of paper, annotate it using the guidelines on pages 15–16.

PEEL your answer

Use PEEL notes to structure your answer (see page 16).

2 Write your answer

Explain the strengths and limitations of any **one** of the indicators in Figure 2 in seeking to understand a country's level of development.

(4 marks)

_____

_____

_____

_____

_____

_____

_____

_____

③ Mark your answer

1. To help you to identify if the answer includes well-structured points, first highlight or underline the:

   - points in red
   - explanations in orange
   - evidence in blue.

2. Use the mark scheme below to decide what mark to give.

Mark scheme

Award marks as follows:

Candidates must explain both a strength and a limitation for their chosen indicator in Figure 2. Possible strengths and weaknesses include:

For HDI:

Strengths include:

- Uses a range of indicators (1) giving a more accurate picture (1).
- Shows how much people benefit (1) from increased GDP (1).

Weaknesses include:

- May not reflect high GDP (1) if wealth is not shared (1).

For death rate per 1000 population:

Strengths include:

- A low figure indicates wealth (1) because it shows people have good health (1).

Weaknesses include:

- May not increase with GDP (1) because a country might not improve health services (1).

For % population with access to safe water:

Strengths include:

- Water quality improves from higher spending (1) as a country becomes affluent (1).

Weaknesses include:

- Some countries like Nigeria do not have high % of safe water (1) because wealth goes to a few and not people as a whole (1).

---

④ Sample answer

Read through Sample answer 3 opposite.

a) Go through it using the three colours in section 3.

b) Decide how many marks it is worth.

Sample answer 3

HDI is a good measure of a country's development, because it shows how well developed a country is socially as well as economically. It is a single figure which combines GDP (to show how wealthy a country is) with literacy (which shows the level of education), and infant mortality (which shows the level of health care). So it is a good way of showing how much money is spent on health and education. A disadvantage is that HDI does not always work in some wealthy countries like Saudi Arabia, because HDI is low as wealth is concentrated in the hands of a few wealthy people, and so does not get spent on people.

5 Marked sample answer 3

Sample answer 3 is marked below. As with sample answers 1 and 2, the text is highlighted as follows:

- points in red
- explanations in orange
- evidence in blue.

Explanation – explains how HDI is useful socially and economically

Evidence – a really clear statement showing the evidence to support the candidate's judgement about HDI

HDI is a good measure of a country's development, because it shows how well developed a country is socially as well as economically. It is a single figure which combines GDP (to show how wealthy a country is) with literacy (which shows the level of education), and infant mortality (which shows the level of health care). So it is a good way of showing how much money is spent on health and education. A disadvantage is that HDI does not always work in some wealthy countries like Saudi Arabia, because HDI is low as wealth is concentrated in the hands of a few wealthy people, and so does not get spent on people.

Point – makes a judgement about health and education

Point – balances the answer with a disadvantage about HDI

Explanation – explains why this is a disadvantage.

✓ Examiner feedback

The candidate knows what HDI is and how it is measured, and can also explain its advantage in combining three measures. Two advantages show how HDI is calculated, and a disadvantage shows why it does not work in countries like Saudi Arabia. In both cases, the candidate refers to evidence to support points made. The answer therefore earns all 4 marks.

On your marks

Getting your head around the 8-mark questions

- **In this section you'll learn how to tackle 8-mark questions using command words 'Assess' and 'Evaluate'.**

8-mark questions – what's different?

8-mark questions differ from 4-mark questions:

- They have tougher command words such as 'Assess', or 'Evaluate'. 4-mark questions tend to use 'Explain' or 'Suggest'.
- They are marked using levels, not points. Levels are criteria (qualities) which examiners look for and use to judge your answer. Level 1 is a lower standard (1–3 marks) and Level 3 is most challenging (worth 7–8 marks).

Getting to grips with 'Assess'

'Assess' means using evidence to decide how significant something is. In a list of possible explanations or actions, you have to consider all of them, then identify which are the most important. For example:

Assess the effectiveness of hard-engineering methods of coastal management.

To 'assess' the effectiveness of these methods, you would have to:

- list the methods of hard engineering that you know
- weigh up how effective each one is
- decide which are most effective and why.

Getting to grips with 'Evaluate'

'Evaluate' means measuring the value or success of something and provide a judgement or conclusion on the basis of evidence, e.g. strengths and weaknesses, or relevant data. For example:

Evaluate the effects of urban regeneration on one named UK city.

To 'evaluate' the effects of regeneration on a city, you have to:

- list the different urban regeneration schemes that you know about
- give examples of which ones have been successful, and why
- give examples of any that have NOT been so successful, and why
- make a judgement – has urban regeneration in this city been successful or not? This would need a short conclusion of one or two sentences.

'Assess' and 'Evaluate' questions in Paper 1

'Assess' and 'Evaluate' questions in Paper 1 are slightly different from those in Paper 2. Those in Paper 1 will not include any stimulus material. They assess:

- your understanding of what you've learned (AO2), which carries 4 marks.
- your ability to apply this through 'assessment' or judgement (AO3), which carries 4 marks.

So simply writing about what you know (AO2) without any assessment or judgement earns a maximum of 4 marks.

Examples of 4- and 8-mark questions

A 4-mark question might ask:

Explain two impacts of human activity on global climate.

An 8-mark question might ask:

Evaluate the statement that 'human activity is causing important changes to global climate'.

Answering 'Assess' and 'Evaluate' questions in Paper 2

8-mark questions in Paper 2 use a resource (e.g. photo, table of data) linked to a question, e.g. fieldwork data in Section C1 or C2. Questions ask you to use the data, and assess or evaluate something about the data.

This means 8 marks are divided into:

- 4 marks AO3, because you'll make a judgement or assessment linked to the question
- 4 marks AO4, because you'll be using geographical skills in interpreting the resource.

Level	Marks	Descriptor (Paper 1)	Descriptor (Paper 2)
	0	No acceptable response.	No acceptable response.
1	1–3	**For AO2** • Shows isolated elements of understanding of concepts and links between places, environments and processes. **For AO3** • Attempts to apply understanding to deconstruct information but understanding and connections are flawed. • An imbalanced or incomplete argument. • Judgements supported by limited evidence.	**For AO3** • Attempts to apply understanding to deconstruct information but understanding and connections are flawed. • An imbalanced or incomplete argument. • Judgements supported by limited evidence. **For AO4** • Uses some geographical skills to obtain information with limited relevance and accuracy, which supports few aspects of the argument.
2	4–6	**For AO2** • Shows elements of understanding of concepts and links between places, environments and processes. **For AO3** • Applies understanding to deconstruct information and give some logical connections between concepts. • An imbalanced argument that draws together some points. • Judgements supported by some evidence.	**For AO3** • Applies understanding to deconstruct information and give some logical connections between concepts. • An imbalanced argument that draws together some points. • Judgements supported by some evidence. **For AO4** • Uses geographical skills to obtain accurate information that supports some aspects of the argument.
3	7–8	**For AO2** • Shows accurate understanding of concepts and links between places, environments and processes. **For AO3** • Applies understanding to deconstruct information and make logical connections between concepts. • A balanced, well-developed argument that draws together relevant points coherently. • Makes judgements supported by evidence.	**For AO3** • Applies understanding to deconstruct information and make logical connections between concepts. • A balanced, well-developed argument that draws together relevant points coherently • Makes judgements supported by evidence. **For AO4** • Uses geographical skills to obtain accurate information that supports all aspects of the argument.

Figure 1 *Marking criteria for all 8-mark questions in Paper 1 and Paper 2 using the command word 'Assess' and Evaluate'. Pages 24–30 and 45–51 use the Paper 1 mark scheme (left); pages 31–44 and pages 52–58 use the Paper 2 mark scheme (right).*

On your marks

8-mark questions using 'Assess' in Paper 1

- **In this section you'll learn how to tackle 8-mark questions which use 'Assess' as a command word in Paper 1.**

Study Figure 1. It shows a street scene in Rocinha favela, a low-income housing area in Rio de Janeiro.

Figure 1

'For those who live in low-income areas of megacities such as Rio de Janeiro, life presents far more problems than benefits'.

Question
Assess the extent to which you agree with the above statement. **(8 marks)**

Five steps to success!

The following five steps are used in this chapter to help you get the best marks.

1
Plan your answer – decide what to include and how to structure your answer.

2
Write your answer – use the answer spaces to complete your answer.

3
Mark your answer – use the mark scheme to self- or peer-mark your answer. You can also use this to assess sample answers in step 4 below.

4
Sample answers – sample answers are given to show you how to maximise marks for a question.

5
Marked sample answers – these are the same answers as for step 4, but are marked and annotated, so that you can compare these with your own.

1 Plan your answer

Before attempting to answer the question, remember to **BUG** it. On a separate piece of paper, annotate it using the guidelines on pages 15–16.

Assess the extent to which you agree with this statement.   **(8 marks)**

Remember!
- 'Assess' in Paper 1 uses your own knowledge and understanding.
- It assesses AO2 (your understanding of a topic) and AO3 (your ability to apply what you know and understand to the question).

PEEL your answer

Use PEEL notes to structure your answer. This will help you to communicate your ideas to the examiner in the clearest way. PEEL has four stages:

- **P**oint – Give at least three pieces of evidence from your megacity study for this question. Use sentences, not bullet points.
- **E**vidence – Include details from named examples of your megacity to support each piece of evidence.
- **E**xplain – Give reasons for each piece of evidence and how it illustrates problems or benefits of living in low-income areas. Use sentence starters such as: '*This is because …*', '*One reason is …*'.
- **L**ink – Link back to the question about whether living in low-income areas of megacities presents more problems than benefits. Finish with a one- or two-sentence conclusion about your judgement.

Planning grid

- Use this planning grid to help you write high-quality paragraphs. Remember to include links to show how your points relate to each other and to the question.
- Note that the fourth row helps you to link back to the question 'assess the extent to which you agree'. Remember – *make a judgement*!

Tip

Make a judgement! Don't just describe and explain. If the question asks you to 'Assess', it wants you to make a judgement. Is it true that *life presents far more problems than benefits … for those who live in low-income areas of megacities*? One way of doing this is in a **mini-conclusion** where you make a judgement – it need only be a sentence or two.

	PEE Paragraph 1	PEE Paragraph 2	PEE Paragraph 3
Point			
Explanation			
Evidence			
How this links back to the question – how far do you agree?			

2 Write your answer

'For those who live in low-income areas of megacities such as Rio de Janeiro, life presents far more problems than benefits'.

Assess the extent to which you agree with this statement.   **(8 marks)**

_____

_____

_____

_____

_____

_____

_____

_____

_____

_____

_____

_____

_____

_____

_____

_____

Strengths of the answer		
Ways to improve the answer		
Level		**Mark**	

3 Mark your answer

1. To help you to identify if the answer includes well-structured points, first highlight or underline the:

   * points in red   * explanations in orange   * evidence in blue
   * points which show the candidate is assessing the statement. These might support one side of the argument, or balance it before reaching a conclusion.

2. Use the mark scheme below. 8-mark questions are not marked using individual points, but choose a level and a mark based upon the quality of the answer as a whole.

Level	Marks	Descriptor	Examples
	0	No acceptable response.	
1	1–3	**For AO2** • Shows isolated elements of understanding of concepts and links between places, environments and processes. **For AO3** • Attempts to apply understanding to deconstruct information but understanding and connections are flawed. • An imbalanced or incomplete argument. • Judgements supported by limited evidence.	• *Developing cities have no water or sewage pipes and have many health problems from drinking bad water.* • *There are so many people that the city cannot keep pace with them all.* • *So the statement is right because life there is very hard and the city cannot support all those people.*
2	4–6	**For AO2** • Shows elements of understanding of concepts and links between places, environments and processes. **For AO3** • Applies understanding to deconstruct information and give some logical connections between concepts. • An imbalanced argument that draws together some points. • Judgements supported by some evidence.	• *Cities like Rio often have no water or sewage connections, and electricity in the photo looks unsafe too.* • *This is because people are poor and cannot afford water or electricity bills* • *So the statement is true because most people do not have a decent lifestyle with basics that we would take for granted.*
3	7–8	**For AO2** • Shows accurate understanding of concepts and links between places, environments and processes. **For AO3** • Applies understanding to deconstruct information and make logical connections between concepts. • A balanced, well-developed argument that draws together relevant points coherently. • Makes judgements supported by evidence.	• *In Rio, a third of homes have no electricity (or have illegal hook-ups from wires like the ones in the photo) and half have no sewage connections.* • *One reason is that favelas like Rocinha are growing so quickly that the city council cannot keep pace with population growth.* • *This shows the statement is true because electricity and sewage connection are basics for a reasonable life. But there are benefits, such as provision of schooling.*

4 Sample answers

Read through Sample answers 1 and 2.

a) Go through each one using the three colours in section 3. Remember to underline points that show the candidate is assessing.

b) Use the level descriptions to decide how many marks each one is worth.

Sample answer 1

I agree with the statement. Rocinha has grown three times its size since 2010. Rio's favelas are growing so quickly that it is hard to keep pace with services like water. It is better than it was because now houses are being built out of brick instead of timber and odd bits of metal, and they also have water and electricity. There are shops there and many services like health facilities that you would expect. But I agree with the statement because Rocinha is probably one of Rio's best favelas and there are many worse that do not have half the benefits that it has. You wouldn't choose to live there if you had more money so areas like that are still for low-income people, so I still think the statement is true.

Elsewhere Rio has squatter settlements, which are places where people just put together their own shacks illegally. Some of these shacks are on sloping land because nobody else wants to live there and they can be a long way from jobs in the city centre. But when it rains heavily, people are vulnerable, because in 2010 over 200 people were killed in a landslide. This shows that the statement is true, because it's the poor have to live there – people with jobs and decent incomes would never choose to live in places like that.

Use a copy of the marking grid below.

Sample answer 2

I don't agree with the statement. It is true that people living in squatter settlements have a lot of problems like they don't have water supply or sewerage connections and when you walk down the street in the photo then you might be electrocuted as the wires don't look very safe. But cities have many jobs for people and so the people who have moved there from the countryside are often employed more than if they had stayed in rural areas. Many rural areas do not have schools and cities like Rio have plenty of schools for all ages maybe universities too. There are often hospitals and medical treatment in cities that you don't have in the countryside. So it's not perfect living in Rio but it can be better than a lot of places so I don't agree with the statement.

Strengths of the answer			
Ways to improve the answer			
Level		Mark	

5 Marked sample answers

Sample answers 1 and 2 are marked below. The following have been highlighted to show how well each answer has structured points.

- points in red
- explanations in orange
- evidence in blue
- judgements are underlined. These are important in order to reach Level 3 on questions whose command word is 'Assess'.

Marked sample answer 1

Point – the candidate quantifies the growth of Rocinha

Explanation – an explanation is given for the impact of this growth

Evidence – the candidate uses the evidence of building materials

Evidence – the candidate uses further evidence of shops and health services

Judgement – the candidate makes a comparison to justify their choice

Judgement – the candidate makes a further statement to justify their choice

Explanation – squatter settlements are explained

Evidence – the candidate uses evidence about land used by squatter settlements

Point – the candidate describes the vulnerability of people

I agree with the statement. Rocinha has grown three times its size since 2010. Rio's favelas are growing so quickly that it is hard to keep pace with services like water. It is better than it was because now houses are being built out of brick instead of timber and odd bits of metal, and they also have water and electricity. There are shops there and many services like health facilities that you would expect. But I agree with the statement because Rocinha is probably one of Rio's best favelas and there are many worse that do not have half the benefits that it has. You wouldn't choose to live there if you had more money so areas like that are still for low-income people, so I still think the statement is true.

Elsewhere Rio has squatter settlements, which are places where people just put together their own shacks illegally. Some of these shacks are on sloping land because nobody else wants to live there and they can be a long way from jobs in the city centre. But when it rains heavily, people are vulnerable because in 2010 over 200 people were killed in a landslide. This shows how the statement is true, because it's the poor have to live there – people with jobs and decent incomes would never choose to live in places like that.

Point – the candidate mentions squatter settlements

Judgement – the candidate gives one further supporting statement to justify their choice, though it is very similar to the second judgement

Explanation – an explanation is given to illustrate this

Examiner feedback

This candidate knows a lot and has a clear view of what living in a favela might be like. The points are well made and the extended points offer detail about favelas to support the answer. The candidate also clearly justifies why they have reached an opinion. The answer is generally Level 3 in quality. However, it is not perfect, as the candidate is short on any data. It is Level 3 and the justification is sound, so it earns 7 marks.

Marked sample answer 2

Point – the candidate makes an illustrated point about squatter settlements

I don't agree with the statement. It is true that people living in squatter settlements have a lot of problems like they don't have water supply or sewerage connections and when you walk down the street in the photo then you might be electrocuted as the wires don't look very safe. But cities have many jobs for people and so the people who have moved there from the countryside are often employed more than if they had stayed in rural areas. Many rural areas do not have schools and cities like Rio have plenty of schools for all ages maybe universities too. There are often hospitals and medical treatment in cities that you don't have in the countryside. So it's not perfect living in Rio but it can be better than a lot of places so I don't agree with the statement.

Evidence – the candidate extends the point using evidence from the photo about electricity

Evidence – the candidate uses evidence of employment to compare cities and rural areas

Point – the candidate makes the point about education in cities

Evidence – the candidate uses the evidence of health care to extend the point further

Point – the candidate makes the point about employment in cities

Judgement – the candidate makes a single statement about living in Rio, though this is not a quality comparison.

Examiner feedback

This is a medium quality answer which was given 5 marks in the middle of Level 2. The candidate makes three valid points about living in squatter settlements and extends it with some detail, but a named city occurs just once in the last sentence. Generic writing, without naming a place, is usually typical of Level 1 – so the candidate has saved themselves by naming Rio twice. The level of judgement is weak; there is no other named place to compare cities with, simply mentioning rural areas.

This candidate probably knows more than this, so some revision of a named city would have earned higher marks – perhaps with some named examples of a megacity they know, or some data illustrating households with water supply etc. Judgement needs to be more than just a general statement at the end.

On your marks

8-mark questions using 'Assess' in Paper 2

- In this section you'll learn how to tackle 8-mark questions which use 'Assess' as a command word in Paper 2.

Study Figure 1, which is a map showing the distribution of Asian Indian British people in London, 2011

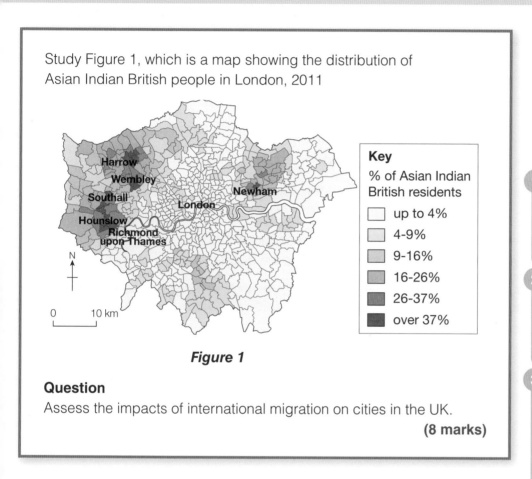

Figure 1

Question

Assess the impacts of international migration on cities in the UK.

(8 marks)

Five steps to success!

The following five steps are used in this chapter to help you get the best marks.

1
Plan your answer – decide what to include and how to structure your answer.

2
Write your answer – use the answer spaces to complete your answer.

3
Mark your answer – use the mark scheme to self- or peer-mark your answer. You can also use this to assess sample answers in step 4 below.

4
Sample answers – sample answers are given to show you how to maximise marks for a question.

5
Marked sample answers – these are the same answers as for step 4, but are marked and annotated, so that you can compare these with your own.

1 Plan your answer

Before attempting to answer the question, remember to **BUG** it. On a separate piece of paper, annotate it using the guidelines on pages 15–16.

Question

Assess the impacts of international migration on cities in the UK.

(8 marks)

Remember!

- 'Assess' is assessed in Paper 2 using a resource stimulus, like the map in this example.
- It assesses AO4 (your skill in interpreting the map) and AO3 (your ability to apply what you see to the question).

PEEL your answer

Use PEEL notes to structure your answer. This will help you to communicate your ideas to the examiner in the clearest way. PEEL has four stages:

- **P**oint – Give at least three pieces of evidence for this question. Use sentences, not bullet points.
- **E**vidence – Include details from named examples to support each piece of evidence.
- **E**xplain – Give reasons for each piece of evidence and how it shows climate is changing. Use sentence starters such as: '*This is because ...*', '*One reason is ...*'.
- **L**ink – Link back to the question about the impacts of international migration on cities in the UK. Finish with a one- or two-sentence conclusion about how big the impacts have been.

Planning grid

Use this planning grid to help you write high-quality paragraphs. Remember to include links to show how your points relate to each other and to the question.

Tip

Make a judgement! Don't just describe and explain. If the question asks you to 'Assess', it wants you to make a judgement. How great have the *impacts of international migration* been *on cities in the UK*? One way of doing this is in a **mini-conclusion** where you make a judgement – it need only be a sentence or two.

	PEE Paragraph 1	PEE Paragraph 2	PEE Paragraph 3
Point			
Explanation			
Evidence (*from map or your own knowledge*)			
Link – a mini conclusion			

2 Write your answer

Assess the impacts of international migration on cities in the UK. **(8 marks)**

_____

_____

_____

_____

_____

_____

_____

_____

_____

_____

_____

_____

_____

_____

_____

_____

_____

_____

Strengths of the answer	
Ways to improve the answer	

Level		**Mark**	

3 Mark your answer

1. To help you to identify if the answer includes well-structured points, first highlight or underline:

   - points in red   • explanations in orange   • evidence in blue
   - any judgements.

2. Use the mark scheme below to decide what mark to give. 8-mark questions are not marked using individual points, but instead you should choose a level and a mark based upon the quality of the answer as a whole.

Level	Marks	Descriptor	Examples
	0	No acceptable response.	
1	1–3	**For AO3** • Tries to apply understanding but understanding and connections are flawed. • Imbalanced or incomplete argument. • Judgements supported by limited evidence. **For AO4** • Uses some geographical skills to obtain information with limited relevance and accuracy.	• *London has a lot of immigrants living there so the city is growing.* • *Immigrants often live in the same sorts of areas where they have their own shops or mosques, and they like living there.*
2	4–6	**For AO3** • Applies understanding to deconstruct information and give some logical connections between concepts. • An imbalanced argument that draws together some points. • Judgements supported by some evidence. **For AO4** • Uses geographical skills to obtain accurate information that supports some of the argument.	• *Immigration has been the reason for half the recent growth of cities such as London. In London there are over 200 languages spoken in the city now.* • *Figure 1 shows that immigrants often settle in suburbs where there are cultural or ethnic groups like their own.*
3	7–8	**For AO3** • Applies understanding to deconstruct information and make logical connections between concepts. • A balanced, well-developed argument that draws together relevant points coherently. • Makes judgements supported by evidence. **For AO4** • Uses geographical skills to obtain accurate information that supports most of the argument.	• *The impacts of immigration have been great especially on the culture of UK cities. In areas like Southall on the map, tourists might be attracted to curry restaurants or shopping at a range of Asian food shops.* • *Figure 1 shows that immigrants from particular countries, religions or cultures tend to live in areas close to each other, creating suburbs like Southall in west London.*

4 Sample answers

Read through Sample answers 1 and 2.

a) Go through each one using the three colours in section 3. Remember to underline any **judgements,** because these are needed to meet the requirements of the command word 'Assess'.

b) Use the level descriptions to decide how many marks it is worth.

Sample answer 1

Half of London's population growth in recent years has been because of migrants from overseas, from countries such as India in Figure 1, because of the jobs available there such as in construction and financial services. International migration has affected London because people from over 200 countries have settled there. Over 37% of the people living in Newham are Asian Indian British residents.

Like the map in Figure 1, many immigrants have changed the character of the parts of the city where they live, because you would probably find shops or places of worship in areas like Wembley. This changes the culture in cities and there are festivals like the Notting Hill Carnival in London. So immigration has had a big effect on cities.

Strengths of the answer			
Ways to improve the answer			
Level		Mark	

Sample answer 2

Cities like London are growing fast because of immigrants from other countries. There are jobs in London which attract people to live there. It has meant that there is pressure on jobs and housing but London gains because there are also new restaurants and festivals which helps the city's image. When migrants arrive they look for work anywhere, but when they get jobs, their families come and join them, so that's what makes the population go up so quickly.

Strengths of the answer			
Ways to improve the answer			
Level		Mark	

⑤ Marked sample answers

Sample answers 1 and 2 are marked below and opposite. The following have been highlighted to show how well each answer has structured points:

- points in red   • explanations in orange   • evidence in blue
- judgements are underlined. These are important in order to reach Level 3 on questions whose command word is 'Assess'.

Marked sample answer 1

Point – candidate quantifies the amount of population growth due to immigration

Evidence – the example of India illustrates the point

Explanation – the reason is given for immigration, i.e. employment (with examples)

Half of London's population growth in recent years has been because of migrants from overseas, from countries such as India in Figure 1, because of the jobs available there such as in construction and financial services. International migration has affected London because people from over 200 countries have settled there. Over 37% of the people living in Newham are Asian Indian British residents.

Like the map in Figure 1, many immigrants have changed the character of the parts of the city where they live, because you would probably find shops or places of worship in areas like Wembley. This changes the culture in cities and there are festivals like the Notting Hill Carnival in London. So immigration has had a big effect on cities.

Point – candidate quantifies the extent of immigration from different countries

Evidence – evidenced with the example of Newham data from Figure 1

Point – the point helps to answer the part of the question dealing with changing character of cities

Explanation – the candidate explains how the character is changed, with examples

Judgement – the candidate makes a judgement about how immigration changes the city. This is not a very strong judgement – but it does fit the command word 'Assess'.

Evidence – candidate illustrates the point with an example

 Examiner feedback

The descriptors for Level 3 apply to this answer as follows:

For AO3:

- *Applies understanding to deconstruct information and make logical connections between concepts.*
- *A balanced, well-developed argument that draws together relevant points coherently.*
- *Makes judgements supported by evidence.*

The candidate has been able to mention both the reasons for growth and the changing character of London. A specific source country is named, data are used, and there is an example of the kind of cultural events resulting from immigration. It does not matter that these examples are chosen from London.

For AO4:

- *Uses geographical skills to obtain accurate information that supports most of the argument.*

This is not so strong. The candidate refers to Figure 1, but only briefly.

By meeting the first descriptor fully, and the second one partly, the answer is low Level 3 in quality. The judgement is also weaker than would be needed for a top Level 3, so the answer is worth 7 marks.

Marked sample answer 2

Point – a general and non-specific point helps to answer the part of the question dealing with growth of cities

Explanation – the candidate briefly explains the reason for growth, but without specific examples

Cities like London are growing fast because of immigrants from other countries. There are jobs in London which attract people to live there. It has meant that there is pressure on jobs and housing but London gains because there are also new restaurants and festivals which help the city's image. When migrants arrive they look for work anywhere, but when they get jobs, their families come and join them, so that's what makes the population go up so quickly.

Explanation – the candidate explains how jobs help to explain immigration but does not offer examples

Point – this point helps to answer the part of the question dealing with changing character of cities

Evidence – candidate evidences the point by showing the benefit of restaurants and festivals

Explanation – the candidate revisits the explanation for growth of population

Note that there are no judgements made in this answer.

 Examiner feedback

The descriptor for Level 1 applies to this answer, as follows:

For AO3:

- *Tries to apply understanding but understanding and connections are flawed.*
- *Imbalanced or incomplete argument.*
- *Judgements supported by limited evidence.*

The candidate quotes patterns from London and clearly understands how important migration, and immigration particularly, are to explain its rapid growth of population. In the latter part of the answer, the candidate also mentions the importance of family members as a reason for further increase. The candidate understands the impact of immigration in terms of food and festivals, but there are no specific examples.

For AO4:

- *Uses some geographical skills to obtain information with limited relevance and accuracy* – the candidate does not refer to Figure 1 at all in the answer – though there are hints of having looked at it.

By meeting the descriptor for Level 1, the answer gains 3 marks.

On your marks

8-mark questions using 'Assess' in Paper 2 Fieldwork

- **In this section you'll learn how to tackle 8-mark questions which use 'Assess' as a command word in the fieldwork section of Paper 2.**

You can use **either** your physical **or** your human fieldwork investigation to answer this question.

> **Question**
> Using the conclusions from your geographical investigation, assess the accuracy and reliability of your results.   **(8 marks)**

1 Plan your answer

Before attempting to answer the question, remember to **BUG** it. That means:
- ✓ **Box** the command word.
- ✓ **Underline** the following:
  - the theme
  - the focus
  - any evidence required
  - the number of examples needed.
- ✓ **Glance** back over the question – to make sure you include everything in your answer.

Annotate the question in the space below.

> Using the conclusions from your geographical investigation, assess the accuracy and reliability of your results.   **(8 marks)**

Five steps to success!

The following five steps are used in this chapter to help you get the best marks.

1 **Plan your answer** – decide what to include and how to structure your answer.

2 **Write your answer** – use the answer spaces to complete your answer.

3 **Mark your answer** – use the mark scheme to self- or peer-mark your answer. You can also use this to assess sample answers in step 4 below.

4 **Sample answers** – sample answers are given to show you how to maximise marks for a question.

5 **Marked sample answers** – these are the same answers as for step 4, but are marked and annotated, so that you can compare these with your own.

Remember!
- 'Assess' makes use of your fieldwork experience and skills, when it is used in the fieldwork section of Paper 2.
- It assesses AO3 (your ability to apply what you experienced to the question) and AO4 (your skill in fieldwork).

PEEL your answer

Use PEEL notes to structure your answer. This will help you to communicate your ideas to the examiner in the clearest way. PEEL has four stages:

- **P**oint – Give at least three pieces of evidence for this question (at least one about accuracy, and one about reliability). Use sentences, not bullet points.
- **E**vidence – Include details from either your physical fieldwork or your human fieldwork to support each piece of evidence.
- **E**xplain – Give reasons for each piece of evidence and how far it shows accuracy or reliability of your results. Use sentence starters such as: '*This is because ...*', '*One reason is ...*'.
- **L**ink – Link back to the question about the accuracy and reliability of your results. Finish with a one- or two-sentence conclusion about how accurate and reliable you were.

> **What's the difference between accuracy and reliability?**
> - **Accuracy** means how carefully you collected results to make sure they were as true as they could be.
> - **Reliability** means that if you went back to the same place on a different day or time, you'd get the same results as you did when you visited.

 Tip

Make a judgement! Don't just describe and explain. The question is asking you to 'Assess', so it wants you to make a judgement. How *accurate* were your fieldwork results? How *reliable* were they? One way of doing this is in a **mini-conclusion** where you make a judgement – it need only be a sentence or two.

Planning grid

Use this planning grid to help you write high-quality paragraphs. Remember to include links to show how your points relate to each other and to the question.

	PEE Paragraph 1	PEE Paragraph 2	PEE Paragraph 3
Point			
Explanation			
Evidence (*from map or your own knowledge*)			
Link – a mini conclusion			

2 Write your answer

Using the conclusions from your geographical investigation, assess the accuracy and reliability of your results. **(8 marks)**

Note: *You can use either your physical or your human fieldwork investigation to answer this question.*

_____

_____

_____

_____

_____

_____

_____

_____

_____

_____

_____

_____

_____

_____

_____

_____

_____

Strengths of the answer	
Ways to improve the answer	

Level		**Mark**	

③ Mark your answer

1. To help you to identify if the answer includes well-structured points, first highlight or underline:

   - points in red   • explanations in orange   • evidence in blue
   - <u>any judgements</u> about accuracy and reliability.

2. Use the mark scheme below to decide what mark to give. 8-mark questions are not marked using individual points, but instead you should choose a level and a mark based upon the quality of the answer as a whole. You'll have to adapt this when marking Sample answer 2 about urban fieldwork.

Level	Marks	Descriptor	Examples
	0	No acceptable response.	
1	1–3	**For AO3** • Tries to apply understanding but understanding and connections are flawed. • Imbalanced or incomplete argument. • Judgements supported by limited evidence. **For AO4** • Few aspects of the enquiry process are supported by the use of geographical skills. • Communicates general fieldwork findings with limited relevance and accuracy and little relevant geographical terminology.	• *We measured width and depth of the river using a tape measure and a ruler.* • *Some of our results weren't accurate because we lost our tape measure and had to use paces.* • *If we went back on another day we'd probably get different results.*
2	4–6	**For AO3** • Applies understanding to deconstruct information and give some logical connections between concepts. • An imbalanced argument that draws together some points. • Judgements supported by some evidence. **For AO4** • Some aspects of the enquiry process are supported by the use of geographical skills. • Communicates fieldwork findings fairly clearly using occasional relevant geographical terminology.	• *We measured the area of the river, then velocity to find volume.* • *Sometimes velocity readings weren't very accurate because our dog biscuit got wet. So I would not trust our volume results as other groups got different results from ours.* • *If we went back on another day it might be drier, so we'd get different results.*
3	7–8	**For AO3** • Applies understanding to deconstruct information and make logical connections between concepts. • A balanced, well-developed argument that draws together relevant points coherently. • Makes judgements supported by evidence. **For AO4** • All aspects of the enquiry process are supported by the use of geographical skills. • Communicates specific fieldwork findings clearly, and consistently uses relevant geographical terminology.	• *Our fieldwork included measuring width and depth of the river, then velocity. Multiplied together, these give discharge calculations, which would vary between one day and another.* • *Our results relied upon each member of each group doing width and depth readings accurately. The group I was with was sometimes a bit rushed, which affected our accuracy.* • *Our readings could not be reliable because the river might have a different discharge on a different day, depending on rainfall.*

4 Sample answers

Read through Sample answers 1 and 2.

a) Go through each one using the three colours in section 3. Remember to underline any **judgements** about accuracy and reliability, because these are needed to answer the question.

b) Use the level descriptions to decide how many marks it is worth.

Sample answer 1 – rivers fieldwork

We measured width, depth and velocity (to calculate discharge) and gradient. The river floods in places, so we used the wider banks of the river to calculate channel capacity at bank-full so that we could calculate how easily it would flood by looking at the maps of flood risk from the Environment Agency. Our BGS phone app also told us the geology and whether rocks are porous or permeable. Both of these were accurate.

Some widths were hard to measure because banks were slippery, making results less accurate. Depth readings varied across the river, so we took several readings and averaged them. We all measured the same sites, but some group results varied perhaps because they didn't do it carefully enough. We took photos so that we could work out which group's results were the accurate ones.

Equipment like flowmeters didn't always work, and gradient was hard to work out using apps on our phones because we didn't want them to get wet. When we did our fieldwork it had rained the day before, so our results would not be reliable compared to a dry summer day. So, in conclusion, we were only partly accurate, and reliability would be difficult depending on the weather.

Use a copy of the marking grid opposite to assess this answer.

Sample answer 2 – urban fieldwork

Generally our results were correct but only in certain ways. We used an environmental quality survey to find out what people living there thought about their area. As long as everyone recorded the data correctly, it would be accurate. But to get a proper picture of the area, we used the Living Environment IMD data, as that's government data and would be reliable.

We also measured noise levels using decibel apps on our phones and counted traffic, which gave a clearer picture of environmental quality and made our results more reliable. It helped when we plotted noise data on a map, as we could see that the noisiest parts were along the main road. You can also tell our results were accurate because everyone said the same thing about litter and graffiti and that it was poor (which it was). We did get different results from different age groups because we collected data in the morning when people were at school and work, so it was mainly old people in one area. That might make our results wrong or misleading.

Strengths of the answer			
Ways to improve the answer			
Level		**Mark**	

5 Marked sample answers

Sample answers 1 and 2 are marked below. The following have been highlighted to show how well each answer has structured points:

- points in red   • explanations in orange   • evidence in blue
- judgements are underlined. These are important in order to reach Level 3 on questions whose command word is 'Assess'.

Marked sample answer 1

Point – identifies a method of data collection

Explanation – extends the point to compare primary with secondary data

Evidence – data collection by the candidate

We measured width, depth and velocity (to calculate discharge) and gradient. The river floods in places, so we used the wider banks of the river to calculate channel capacity at bank-full so that we could calculate how easily it would flood by looking at the maps of flood risk from the Environment Agency. Our BGS phone app also told us the geology and whether rocks are porous or permeable. Both of these were accurate.

Judgement – links back to the question, though the candidate does not say why the data are accurate

Some widths were hard to measure because banks were slippery, making results less accurate. Depth readings varied across the river, so we took several readings and averaged them. We all measured the same sites, but some group results varied perhaps because they didn't do it carefully enough. We took photos so that we could work out which group's results were the accurate ones.

Point – identifies a problem with data accuracy

Explanation – extends the point to explain how the problem was resolved

Evidence – evidence is given of further inaccuracy

Equipment like flowmeters didn't always work, and gradient was hard to work out using apps on our phones because we didn't want them to get wet. When we did our fieldwork it had rained the day before, so our results would not be reliable compared to a dry summer day. So, in conclusion, we were only partly accurate, and reliability would be difficult depending on the weather.

Judgement – links back to the question, explaining how greater accuracy was achieved

Point – identifies equipment accuracy as a problem

Explanation – explains why reliability is a problem

Judgement – links back to the question, making a judgement

Evidence – an example of reliability

✓ **Examiner feedback**

See feedback on page 44.

Marked sample answer 2

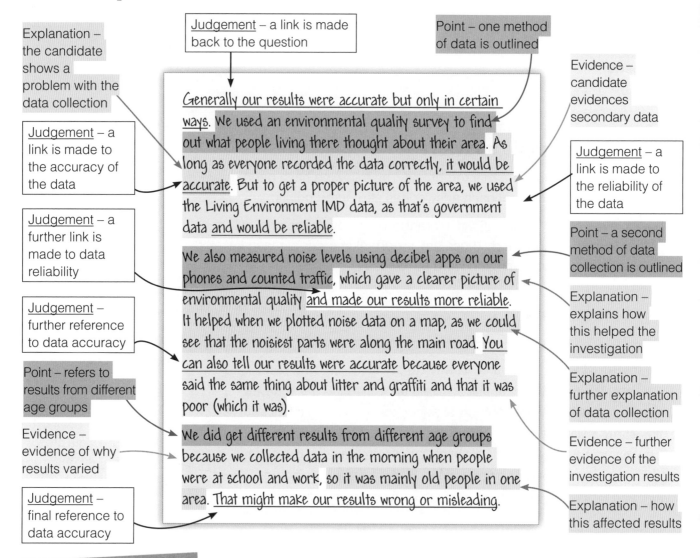

Explanation – the candidate shows a problem with the data collection

Judgement – a link is made back to the question

Point – one method of data is outlined

Evidence – candidate evidences secondary data

Judgement – a link is made to the accuracy of the data

Judgement – a link is made to the reliability of the data

Judgement – a further link is made to data reliability

Point – a second method of data collection is outlined

Judgement – further reference to data accuracy

Explanation – explains how this helped the investigation

Point – refers to results from different age groups

Explanation – further explanation of data collection

Evidence – evidence of why results varied

Evidence – further evidence of the investigation results

Judgement – final reference to data accuracy

Explanation – how this affected results

> Generally our results were accurate but only in certain ways. We used an environmental quality survey to find out what people living there thought about their area. As long as everyone recorded the data correctly, it would be accurate. But to get a proper picture of the area, we used the Living Environment IMD data, as that's government data and would be reliable.
>
> We also measured noise levels using decibel apps on our phones and counted traffic, which gave a clearer picture of environmental quality and made our results more reliable. It helped when we plotted noise data on a map, as we could see that the noisiest parts were along the main road. You can also tell our results were accurate because everyone said the same thing about litter and graffiti and that it was poor (which it was).
>
> We did get different results from different age groups because we collected data in the morning when people were at school and work, so it was mainly old people in one area. That might make our results wrong or misleading.

✓ **Examiner feedback**

The descriptors for Level 3 applies to both answers as follows:

For AO3:

- Applies understanding to deconstruct information and make logical connections between concepts.
- A balanced, well-developed argument that draws together relevant points coherently.
- Makes judgements supported by evidence.

The candidate has been able to mention both accuracy and reliability in these investigations. Three issues that refer to evidence are explored in both answers, and there are examples of real fieldwork which are explained in detail. Links are made back to the questions and both answers are top quality assessments of each investigation.

For AO4:

- Uses geographical skills to obtain accurate information that supports most of the argument.

This is also strong in both answers. The candidate refers to specific methods of data collection.

By meeting all descriptors fully, both answers are top Level 3 in quality, and are worth all 8 marks.

On your marks

8-mark questions using 'Evaluate' in Paper 1

- In this section you'll learn how to tackle 8-mark questions which use 'Evaluate' as a command word in Paper 1.

> **Question**
> Evaluate the evidence that suggests that the global climate is currently changing.   **(8 marks)**

1 Plan your answer

Before attempting to answer the question, remember to **BUG** it. That means:

✓ **Box** the command word.
✓ **Underline** the following:
  - the theme
  - the focus
  - any evidence required
  - the number of examples needed.
✓ **Glance** back over the question – to make sure you include everything in your answer.

Use the BUG below to plan your own answer.

Command word: 'Evaluate' means 'judge on its strengths and weaknesses'. You need to decide whether evidence is strong or weak.

Evidence: Use evidence from your own knowledge and understanding, such as shrinking glaciers and seasonal weather changes.

Evaluate the evidence that suggests that the global climate is currently changing. **(8 marks)**

Focus and number of examples: The focus is evidence for a changing global climate. For an 8-mark question, you need three points which are well developed. Each piece of evidence needs to be written in a paragraph. You also need a mini-conclusion.

Theme: Climate change is linked to the theme *Hazardous Earth*, assessed in Paper 1, Section A of your exam. The question is compulsory.

Remember!
- 'Evaluate' is assessed in Paper 1 using your own knowledge and understanding.
- It assesses AO2 (your understanding of a topic) and AO3 (your ability to apply what you know and understand to the question, and make a judgement).

Five steps to success!

The following five steps are used in this chapter to help you get the best marks.

1 Plan your answer – decide what to include and how to structure your answer.

2 Write your answer – use the answer spaces to complete your answer.

3 Mark your answer – use the mark scheme to self- or peer-mark your answer. You can also use this to assess sample answers in step 4 below.

4 Sample answers – sample answers are given to show you how to maximise marks for a question.

5 Marked sample answers – these are the same answers as for step 4, but are marked and annotated, so that you can compare these with your own.

PEEL your answer

Use PEEL notes to structure your answer. This will help you to communicate your ideas to the examiner in the clearest way. PEEL has four stages:

- **P**oint – Give at least three pieces of evidence for this question. Use sentences, not bullet points.
- **E**vidence – Include details from named examples to support each piece of evidence.
- **E**xplain – Give reasons for each piece of evidence and how it shows climate is changing. Use sentence starters such as: '*This is because …*', '*One reason is …*'.
- **L**ink – Link back to the question about how reliable the evidence is. Finish it off with a one- or two-sentence conclusion about how strong the evidence is that climate is changing.

Tip

Evaluate means stating how strong each piece of evidence is

Don't just describe and explain; show the strength of research behind it. For example, the *changing global climate* might by about shrinking glaciers or increased storminess. You need to say whether this is strong evidence or not. Then draw it together, in a **mini-conclusion** – it need only be a sentence or two.

Planning grid

Use this planning grid to help you write high-quality paragraphs. Remember to include links to show how your points relate to each other and to the question.

Note that the fourth row helps you to focus on 'evaluate' – to **evaluate the evidence**.

	PEE Paragraph 1	PEE Paragraph 2	PEE Paragraph 3
Point			
Explanation			
Evidence (*from your own knowledge*)			
Evaluation of the evidence			

2 Write your answer

Evaluate the evidence that suggests that the global climate is currently changing.　　**(8 marks)**

Strengths of the answer	
Ways to improve the answer	
Level		Mark	

3 Mark your answer

1. To help you to identify if the answer includes well-structured points, first highlight or underline:

   - points in red   • explanations in orange   • evidence in blue
   - links to the question that show evaluation.

2. Use the mark scheme below to decide what mark to give. 8-mark questions are not marked using individual points, but instead you should choose a level and a mark based upon the quality of the answer as a whole.

Level	Marks	Descriptor	Examples
	0	No acceptable response.	
1	1–3	**For AO2** • Shows isolated elements of understanding of concepts and links between places, environments and processes. **For AO3** • Attempts to apply understanding to deconstruct information but understanding and connections are flawed. • An imbalanced or incomplete argument. • Judgements supported by limited evidence.	• *World temperatures are going up all the time and winters are getting warmer.* • *Global warming is making the seasons different and there are more floods.* • *Scientists think more floods and storms are caused by global warming.*
2	4–6	**For AO2** • Shows elements of understanding of concepts and links between places, environments and processes. **For AO3** • Applies understanding to deconstruct information and give some logical connections between concepts. • An imbalanced argument that draws together some points. • Judgements supported by some evidence.	• *Scientists show that global sea levels have risen in the past 100 years.* • *This is due to global warming which increases temperatures and melts ice caps and glaciers, which go into the sea.* • *We know sea level is rising because countries with coastlines are getting flooded.*
3	7–8	**For AO2** • Shows accurate understanding of concepts and links between places, environments and processes. **For AO3** • Applies understanding to deconstruct information and make logical connections between concepts. • A balanced, well-developed argument that draws together relevant points coherently. • Makes judgements supported by evidence.	• *IPCC research shows that average global sea level has risen by 10–20 cm since 1920.* • *This is probably due to rising global temperatures which melt ice caps, so more water goes into the sea.* • *This is likely to be reliable evidence as the IPCC consists of thousands of the world's best scientists.*

4 Sample answers

Read through Sample answers 1 and 2.

a) Go through each one using the three colours in section 3, including underlining any evaluative points.

b) Use the level descriptions to decide how many marks it is worth.

Sample answer 1

Many sources of evidence show how climate is changing. Temperatures have risen globally by about 0.8 °C since the 19th century. This is probably due to carbon emissions of greenhouse gases like CO_2 from burning fossil fuels.

Temperatures seem to be getting warmer all the time, so that sea level will carry on rising. Already some islands in the Pacific have been flooded and countries like Bangladesh have severe floods because much of the country is very low lying. Glaciers in mountains like the Himalayas have been melting because temperatures are rising, so that this all goes to the sea via rivers and makes sea level rise.

Another piece of evidence is that the seasons seem to be changing, so that spring is earlier, and winters are not as cold as they were, and have less snow. Birds migrate earlier than they did and their nests are being built nine days earlier than forty years ago. So that all seems to mean that there is a lot of evidence that climate is changing.

Use a copy of the marking grid below to assess this answer.

Sample answer 2

Globally the climate is warming, and there is evidence to prove that this is the case. Global temperatures are 1 °C warmer than they were 100 years ago because greenhouse gas emissions have increased. It is hard to know exactly what temperatures were like in 1900, and more people and organisations record the weather now than at that time, but there were thermometers, just fewer of them. So, some of the evidence could be questionable, because there were fewer recordings.

Even if temperature recordings are not completely reliable, there is a lot of evidence to show that sea level has risen globally by about 20 cm in 100 years, partly because ocean water expands when it warms and so it rises. Many coastal areas are flooding more now, so it is a global process and not just evidence from one place.

Other evidence that shows temperatures are rising comes from retreating glaciers and ice sheets because they are melting. Many glaciers have been photographed for over 100 years, and many in the Alps and on Greenland show that they have retreated a long way from where they once were.

Strengths of the answer		
Ways to improve the answer		
Answer Level		Mark	

⑤ Marked sample answers

Sample answers 1 and 2 are marked below. The following have been highlighted to show how well each answer has structured points:

- points in red
- explanations in orange
- evidence in blue
- evaluations are underlined. These are important to reach Level 3 on questions whose command word is 'Evaluate'.

Marked sample answer 1

> Many sources of evidence show how climate is changing. Temperatures have risen globally by about 0.8 °C since the 19th century. This is probably due to carbon emissions of greenhouse gases like CO_2 from burning fossil fuels.
>
> Temperatures seem to be getting warmer all the time, so that sea level will carry on rising. Already some islands in the Pacific have been flooded and countries like Bangladesh have severe floods because much of the country is very low lying. Glaciers in mountains like the Himalayas have been melting because temperatures are rising, so that this all goes to the sea via rivers and makes sea level rise.
>
> Another piece of evidence is that the seasons seem to be changing, so that spring is earlier, and winters are not as cold as they were, and have less snow. Birds migrate earlier than they did and their nests are being built nine days earlier than forty years ago. So that all seems to mean that there is a lot of evidence that climate is changing.

Point – quantifying the amount of warming

Explanation – a reason is given for warming of the global climate

Point – the candidate offers further evidence

Explanation – a reason is given for flooding in many countries

Point – further evidence is given for climate change

Evidence – the candidate discusses retreating glaciers as evidence for rising sea levels

Point – further evidence; winters are warmer now

Explanation – a reason is given for glaciers melting

Evidence – the point is extended with the example of bird migrations

 Examiner feedback

Examiners often see this kind of answer. This candidate knows a lot and has learned facts and figures. The answer is a problem though, because there is no evaluation. The candidate needs to ask themselves – *'what's the evidence that glaciers are melting, and is it reliable? How do I know it's reliable?'*.

The answer is therefore a mix of levels:

- Almost Level 3 for AO2, understanding climate change and global warming.
- Explanations are mid-Level 2 because they do not always link to warming climate (e.g. flooding in Bangladesh is explained because it is low lying, not because of sea level change).
- However, there is no evaluation, an essential quality for high Level 2 or Level 3.

Faced with this, examiners have to do a 'best fit' or a kind of average. The examiner gives this low Level 2 and 4 marks.

Marked sample answer 2

Explanation – the candidate briefly explains the increase in temperatures

Point – the candidate makes the point about increasing temperatures

Globally the climate is warming, and there is evidence to prove that this is the case. Global temperatures are 1 °C warmer than they were 100 years ago because greenhouse gas emissions have increased. It is hard to know exactly what temperatures were like in 1900, and more people and organisations record the weather now than at that time, but there were thermometers, just fewer of them. So, some of the evidence could be questionable, because there were fewer recordings.

Even if temperature recordings are not completely reliable, there is a lot of evidence to show that sea level has risen globally by about 20 cm in 100 years, partly because ocean water expands when it warms and so it rises. Many coastal areas are flooding more now, so it is a global process and not just evidence from one place.

Other evidence that shows temperatures are rising comes from retreating glaciers and ice sheets because they are melting. Many glaciers have been photographed for over 100 years, and many in the Alps and on Greenland show that they have retreated a long way from where they once were.

Evaluation – one reason given why temperature readings may not be accurate

Evaluation – the evaluation is extended by referring to volume of temperature recordings

Point – a second point about rising sea level

Explanation – the candidate gives a reason for this

Evaluation – the candidate shows that this is probably reliable as many places experience the same thing

Point – a point about retreating glaciers

Evaluation – reference to the reliability of photos taken over a long time to show change

Explanation – the candidate explains the point about retreating glaciers

 Examiner feedback

This is a top quality answer which was given the full 8 marks.

Notice that the candidate giving this answer has shown less knowledge and understanding (AO2) than the candidate giving Sample answer 1, but nearly half of the answer is spent showing whether the evidence for change is reliable or not (AO3). That's what you need to do in a question whose command word is 'Evaluate'. Spend as much time on evaluating as you do in showing your knowledge and understanding.

On your marks

8-mark questions using 'Evaluate' in Paper 2

- **In this section you'll learn how to tackle 8-mark questions which use 'Evaluate' as a command word in Paper 2.**

Study Figure 1, a photo showing deposition of sediment along a stretch of coast in South Australia.

Figure 1

Question
Using Figure 1, evaluate the part played by sediment deposition in creating coastal landscapes. **(8 marks plus 4 marks SPaG)**

Five steps to success!

The following five steps are used in this chapter to help you get the best marks.

1 Plan your answer – decide what to include and how to structure your answer.

2 Write your answer – use the answer spaces to complete your answer.

3 Mark your answer – use the mark scheme to self- or peer-mark your answer. You can also use this to assess sample answers in step 4 below.

4 Sample answer – sample answer shows you how to maximise marks for a question.

5 Marked sample answer – this is the same answer as for step 4, but is marked and annotated, so that you can compare with your own.

How is SPaG assessed?

One 8-mark question on each of Papers 1 and 2 will assess spelling, punctuation, grammar and the use of specialist terminology (SPaG); 4 marks are allocated as follows:

- high performance (4 marks)
- intermediate performance (2–3 marks)
- threshold performance (1 mark).

Examiners mark SPaG based on your:

- spelling accuracy, including capitalisation
- punctuation – the use of commas, full stops and semi-colons. Try reading an answer aloud; if it leaves you gasping for breath, it needs more punctuation!
- syntax – i.e. the quality of your grammar
- use of paragraphs.

Level	Marks	Descriptor
	0	Writes nothing or in a style which does not link to the question, or make sense of the question.
1	1	Spelling and punctuation reasonably accurate. Some meaning overall. A limited range of specialist terms.
2	2–3	Spelling and punctuation show considerable accuracy. Grammar shows general control of meaning overall with a good range of specialist terms.
3	4	Spelling and punctuation show consistent accuracy. Grammar shows effective control of meaning overall with a wide range of specialist terms.

Figure 2 Mark scheme for SPaG

1 Plan your answer

Before attempting to answer the question, remember to **BUG** it using the guidelines on pages 15–16.

Annotate the question in the space below.

> **Remember!**
> * 'Evaluate' is assessed in Paper 2 using a resource stimulus, like the photo in this example.
> * It assesses AO4 (your skill in interpreting the photo) and AO3 (your ability to apply what you see to the question.

> Using Figure 1, evaluate the part played by sediment deposition in creating coastal landscapes. **(8 marks, plus 4 marks SPaG)**

PEEL your answer

Use PEEL notes to structure your answer. This will help you to communicate your ideas to the examiner in the clearest way. PEEL has four stages:

* **P**oint – Give at least three pieces of evidence for this question.
  Use sentences, not bullet points.
* **E**vidence – Include details from the photo to support each piece of evidence.
* **E**xplain – Give reasons for each piece of evidence and how sediment deposition creates coastal landscapes.
  Use sentence starters such as: '*This is because ...*', '*One reason is ...*'.
* **L**ink – Link back to the question about ways in which sediment contributes to coastal landscapes. Finish it off with a one- or two-sentence conclusion about the contribution that sediment deposition can make.

 Tip

Evaluate means stating how strong each piece of evidence is.

Don't just describe and explain: show the strength of evidence. For example, if a coastal spit is the most significant feature along a stretch of coast, then sediment deposition makes a big contribution. Draw your argument together in a **mini-conclusion** – it need only be a sentence or two.

Planning grid

Use this planning grid to help you write high-quality paragraphs.
Remember to include links to show how your points relate to each other
and to the question. Note that this is an 8-mark question, so needs three
PEE Paragraphs.

Note that the fourth row helps you to focus on 'evaluate' – to **evaluate the evidence**.

	PEE Paragraph 1	PEE Paragraph 2	PEE Paragraph 3
Point			
Explanation			
Evidence (*from your own knowledge*)			
Evaluation of the evidence			

2 Write your answer

Using Figure 1, evaluate the part played by sediment deposition in creating coastal landscapes.

(8 marks, plus 4 marks SPaG)

Strengths of the answer	
Ways to improve the answer	

Level		Mark	

③ Mark your answer

1. To help you to identify if the answer includes well-structured points, first highlight or underline:

   - points in red   • explanations in orange   • evidence in blue
   - links to the question that show evaluation.

2. Use the mark scheme below to decide what mark to give. 8-mark questions are not marked using individual points, but instead you should choose a level and a mark based upon the quality of the answer as a whole.

3. Remember to give a mark for SPaG!

Level	Marks	Descriptor	Examples
	0	No acceptable response.	
1	1–3	**For AO3** • Attempts to apply understanding to deconstruct information but understanding and connections are flawed. • An imbalanced or incomplete argument. • Judgements supported by limited evidence. **For AO4** • Uses some geographical skills to obtain information with limited relevance and accuracy, which supports few aspects of the argument.	• *The spit comes from waves which break on the beach and longshore drift takes place.* • *The photo shows a sandy beach which reaches almost across the river.* • *Deposition creates many features like spits and beaches.*
2	4–6	**For AO3** • Applies understanding to deconstruct information and give some logical connections between concepts. • An imbalanced argument that draws together some points. • Judgements supported by some evidence. **For AO4** • Uses geographical skills to obtain accurate information that supports some aspects of the argument.	• *Coastal spits are formed when waves break on the shore at an angle and take sediment along the coast forming a long, sandy headland into the water.* • *Figure 1 shows how the river stops the spit from forming a bar which would join the two bits of coast together. So deposition can create important landforms.* • *There might be many coastal deposits along a coast, like sandy beaches which lead to resorts like Brighton.*
3	7–8	**For AO3** • Applies understanding to deconstruct information and make logical connections between concepts. • A balanced, well-developed argument that draws together relevant points coherently. • Makes judgements supported by evidence. **For AO4** • Uses geographical skills to obtain accurate information that supports all aspects of the argument.	• *The coastal spit shown has been formed by two sets of processes. The main one is longshore drift, caused by winds creating waves which hit the shore at an angle.* • *Figure 1 shows a coastal spit which has forced the river to divert from where it used to reach the sea. This shows the impact of sediment – it can divert features such as rivers.* • *Spits are really significant landforms, like Spurn Head in East Yorkshire which shelters the Humber from storms.*

4 Sample answer

Read through the sample answer below.

a) Go through it using the three colours in section 3, including underlining any evaluative points.

b) Use the level descriptions to decide how many marks it is worth.

The photo shows a spit formed of sand that has been deposited on the beach. The waves approach at an angle and swash takes the sand up the beach, where it runs back down in a zig-zag pattern. Further waves repeat the process, so an elongated spit is formed. The spit in the photo moved until it reached the river, and the river current has then shaped it where it runs out to sea. The river in the photo has been diverted around the spit. Deposition can therefore divert river flow, showing how important it is.

Another depositional landform is a sand bar, which is like a spit except that there is no river to prevent movement of sand. The bar develops until it cuts off a lagoon. The lagoon can create important wildlife refuges because freshwater behind the bar remains sheltered and ideal for wildfowl, especially in winter. This means that deposition can create important features of coastal landscapes, like mud flats behind a spit, which are areas of calm water away from storms.

The final contribution made by coastal deposition is beaches, which have physical impacts because they protect cliffs from erosion by absorbing friction from advancing waves. Where longshore drift moves beach material away, it may increase coastal retreat.

Strengths of the answer	
Ways to improve the answer	

Level		Mark out of 8	
SPaG level		Mark out of 4	

5 Marked sample answer

The sample answer is marked on the next page. The following have been highlighted to show how well each answer has structured points:

- points in red
- explanations in orange
- evidence in blue
- links to the question that show evaluation are underlined.

Explanation – the process is described by which the spit forms

Point – identifies a spit and makes it clear it's depositional

Evidence – the candidate evidences the process from the photo. This kind of evidence is important when you need to explain processes as a sequence of stages

The photo shows a spit formed of sand that has been deposited on the beach. The waves approach at an angle and swash takes the sand up the beach, where it runs back down in a zig-zag pattern. Further waves repeat the process, so an elongated spit is formed. The spit in the photo moves until it reached the river, and the river current has then shaped it where it runs out to sea. The river in the photo has been diverted around the spit. Deposition can therefore divert river flow, showing how important it is.

Link – shows the importance of depositional features (evaluation)

Another depositional landform is a sand bar, which is like a spit except that there is no river to prevent movement of sand. The bar develops until it cuts off a lagoon. The lagoon can create important wildlife refuges because freshwater behind the bar remains sheltered and ideal for wildfowl, especially in winter. This means that deposition can create important features of coastal landscapes, like mud flats behind a spit, which are areas of calm water away from storms.

Point – identifies a sand bar and makes it clear it's depositional

Explanation – the process of bar formation is explained

The final contribution made by coastal deposition is beaches, which have physical impacts because they protect cliffs from erosion by absorbing friction from advancing waves. Where longshore drift moves beach material away, it may increase coastal retreat.

Link – uses wording of the question about the importance of features of landscapes (evaluation)

Evidence – exemplifies mud flats as important features

Explanation – the importance of beaches is explained

Point – beaches are named as a third depositional landform

 Examiner feedback

This is a good answer. This candidate explains three landforms, and uses the photo to identify features. The photo is used in the first paragraph, but not afterwards, so AO4 is less here than AO3, where the candidate shows some good explanation. The answer needs a final mini-conclusion in the last sentence.

The descriptors for Level 3 for AO2 applies to this answer:

- *'Applies understanding to deconstruct information and make logical connections between concepts'* – the candidate shows an ability to describe landform formation in some detail. Landforms are identified and processes described.
- *'.... A balanced, well-developed argument that draws together relevant points coherently'* – the candidate develops an argument to show how important deposition is.
- *'Makes judgements supported by evidence'* – the candidate refers to the photo meaningfully, firstly by naming the landforms, and secondly by explaining the significance of the landforms.

Because the photo is not referred to much in the answer, the descriptor for Level 2 for AO4 applies:

- *Uses geographical skills to obtain accurate information that supports some aspects of the argument* – more use could be made of the photo.

The mark given is therefore a best fit between AO3 and AO4, so the candidate is given 6 marks.

For SPaG, the answer is given 4 marks – spelling, syntax, and paragraphing are all good.

On your marks

Hitting the high marks on 12-mark questions in Paper 3

- **In this section you will learn how to prepare for the 12-mark questions in Paper 3, which use the command word 'Justify'.**

What's different about Paper 3?

Paper 3 is different from Papers 1 and 2.

- It is a decision-making exercise (DME) about a geographical issue assessing the biosphere (Topic 7) and resources (Topic 9), focusing on a place which will be located in either a taiga or tropical rainforest region (Topic 8).
- The issue will be given to you in a Resource Booklet (of about 10 pages). It will probably be about a place that you haven't studied. Don't worry about this – it is your ability to read and interpret the booklet that is being assessed, not your knowledge of the place.
- The exam lasts for 1 hour 30 minutes. It has a total of 64 marks, including 4 marks for spelling, punctuation, grammar and use of specialist terminology (SPaG). This means it's less pressured for time than the other papers.
- The last question will ask you to make a decision about the issue in the Resource Booklet. That will need thinking and planning time – that's why the timing of the paper is different.

Spending your time in the exam

- It's essential that you read the Resource Booklet carefully, so that you become familiar with the information.
- The Resource Booklet will give you information about the issue and the place, and will lead up to proposals for the future. It will contain text, maps, photographs, graphs, tables of data, and views and opinions about the issue.
- Use these resources to help you make sense of the place and the issue.
- Most exam questions will test your understanding of the booklet, though some will test your wider understanding of Topics 7, 8 and 9.
- Some of the questions will involve making calculations, so you'll have access to a calculator.

Preparing for Paper 3

Both the Resource Booklet and exam paper are organised into sections:

- Section A: People and the biosphere (Topic 7)
- Section B: Forests under threat (Topic 8)
- Section C: Consuming energy resources (Topic 9)
- Section D: Making a geographical decision (Topics 7, 8 and 9)

To prepare for the exam, you will need to revise all three topics, because some shorter questions will test your knowledge and understanding of them (AO2). You will also need to apply your knowledge and understanding (AO2) along with interpreting information in the Resource Booklet (AO4).

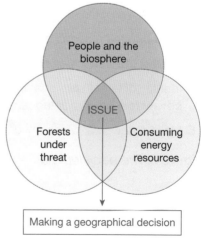

Figure 1 *How Topics 7, 8 and 9 link together*

Recipes for success in Paper 3

The exam paper will always have the same format (Figure 2).

Paper 3: **People and environment issues – Making a geographical decision** You'll be given a Resource Booklet Total marks: **64 including 4 marks for SPaG** Weighting: **25%** Time: **1 hr 30 mins**	**Section A: People and the biosphere** • Marked out of 8. • Answer all questions in Section A.
	Section B: Forests under threat • Marked out of 7. • Answer all questions in Section B.
	Section C: Consuming energy resources • Marked out of 33, including two 8-mark questions. • Answer all questions in Section C.
	Section D: Making a geographical decision • The decision will be about an energy issue in either tropical rainforest or taiga. • One 12-mark question plus 4 marks SPaG (16 marks).

Figure 2 *The format of Paper 3*

The questions in the examination follow a decision-making process (Figure 3). They're not separate, but linked into a sequence.

- The issue is stated at the start of the Resource Booklet.
- Read the booklet first and then think about the issue.
- The most demanding question is in Section D, where you'll have to justify a choice from three options.
- There is no preferred option among examiners. All options can be justified. Your reasons for making a choice will vary according to the chosen option.
- It's marked by assessing a mix of AO2 (understanding from the course), AO3 (applying and developing your argument), and AO4 (skill in selecting information from the Resource Booklet).

Stage	Where you can find this in the exam
1 Identify a problem or a need.	Section A
2 Exploring the reasons for the problem.	Section B
3 Look at the issues behind the problem.	Section C
4 Identify different solutions/options and weigh up advantages/ disadvantages.	Section D
5 Make a decision: which option is best?	Section D

Figure 3 *The decision-making process*

How to justify an argument in Section D

To do well on the 12-mark question, your answer will need to:

- make a clear choice of one option
- explain its impact on the economy, people and environment
- weigh up advantages/disadvantages of all three options
- make an overall judgement.

To make a choice, consider the following:

Economic factors

- Will the number of jobs increase, including those which are higher skilled, higher paid?
- Will there be an Increase in GDP?
- Will the area become more attractive for investment?

Social

- Will people's quality of life improve?
- Will there be better housing, health and education?

Environmental

- Will air and water quality improve/reduce pollution?
- Will wildlife be protected/conserved?
- Will the built environment be improved?

Checklist

- Have you written about all three options?
- Have you given a clear argument justifying your choice of the best option? You need at least two advantages, and two disadvantages explaining why you rejected the other two options. (AO3)
- Have you given detailed evidence from the booklet? (AO4)
- Have you included some knowledge and understanding from Topic 7 (People and the biosphere) to Topic 9 (Consuming energy resources)? (AO2)

Writing a top quality answer

Read the following answer to the question opposite (it is question 4 on page 157 of this book). Using highlighters, pick out where the candidate has:

- put together an argument (AO3)
- picked out detail from the Resource Booklet (AO4)
- used information that isn't in the booklet but the candidate has learned from the rest of the course (AO2).

In pairs, come to a mark out of 12 and for SPaG. Check your verdict with the marked example on the next page.

Question

Study the **three** options below for how the DRC should provide sufficient energy to provide for its population and form the basis of the development of the country in the 21st century. (16 marks)

The DRC government faces many challenges. It needs energy to develop, but has the problem of severe environmental impacts. DRC's population is growing fast, because death rates are low while birth rates remain high (Figures 7, 8, 9). It needs to grow economically to sustain its population, to grow crops to feed them, and also employment. Option 1 can provide these.

Option 1 is most suitable as it allows economic development while protecting remaining rainforests. This is because the government would be able to attract new industries with existing energy resources, and also benefit from the economic multiplier effect of new jobs, and from the REDD scheme attracting money from Norway because DRC would be protecting its rainforests from further destruction. This would be needed, because rainforest destruction through the Inga dams (Figure 14) is enormous, and they need to prevent further damage.

Socially, Option 1 would benefit forest indigenous peoples. Figure 11 shows the benefits that people gain from the rainforest, e.g. food, medicines. Their lives depend on the forest, from crops to hunting and gathering. This has the potential for ecotourism, as does Option 2, as people would want to see traditional lifestyles, which are disappearing across the world as rainforests are destroyed. Tourist development would also increase the economic multiplier.

I rejected Option 2, though it came close second. Rainforests should be replanted, but the only way DRC will develop in future is if energy resources are plentiful. That's the benefit of Option 1. Some African countries are starting to develop economically because labour costs are cheap compared to other countries, and they need to develop economically so that they gain through jobs. Option 2 feels like development would be small scale.

I rejected Option 3 because it would destroy rainforest, and DRC would receive no income from Norway for maintaining forests. Clearance would also remove carbon sinks and increase the percentage of greenhouse gases in the atmosphere, leading to faster climate change. It would acidify water in the dams as rainforests rotted below water level. It seems to have no advantages.

To conclude, Option 1 is best for where DRC is now. Energy is needed but not as Option 3 suggests.

Marked example

Read the annotations below.

- Introduction and conclusions are <u>underlined.</u>
- Parts of the argument (AO3) are shown in red.
- Details from the Resource Booklet (AO4) are shown in blue.
- information learned from the rest of the course (AO2) is in orange.

<u>The DRC government faces many challenges. It needs energy to develop, but has the problem of severe environmental impacts.</u> DRC's population is growing fast, because death rates are low while birth rates remain high (Figures 7, 8, 9). <u>It needs to grow economically to sustain its population, to grow crops to feed them, and also employment. Option 1 can provide these.</u>

Option 1 is most suitable as it allows economic development while protecting remaining rainforests. This is because the government would be able to attract new industries with existing energy resources, and also benefit from the economic multiplier effect of new jobs, and from the REDD scheme attracting money from Norway because DRC would be protecting its rainforests from further destruction. This would be needed, because rainforest destruction through the Inga dams (Figure 14) is enormous, and they need to prevent further damage.

Socially, Option 1 would benefit forest indigenous peoples. Figure 11 shows the benefits that people gain from the rainforest, e.g. food, medicines. Their lives depend on the forest, from crops to hunting and gathering. This has the potential for ecotourism, as does Option 2, as people would want to see traditional lifestyles, which are disappearing across the world as rainforests are destroyed. Tourist development would also increase the economic multiplier.

I rejected Option 2, though it came close second. Rainforests should be replanted, but the only way DRC will develop in future is if energy resources are plentiful. That's the benefit of Option 1. Some African countries are starting to develop economically because labour costs are cheap compared to other countries, and they need to develop economically so that they gain through jobs. Option 2 feels like development would be small scale.

I rejected Option 3 because it would destroy rainforest, and DRC would receive no income from Norway for maintaining forests. Clearance would also remove carbon sinks and increase the percentage of greenhouse gases in the atmosphere, leading to faster climate change. It would acidify water in the dams as rainforests rotted below water level. It seems to have no advantages.

<u>To conclude, Option 1 is best for where DRC is now. Energy is needed but not as Option 3 suggests.</u>

 Examiner decision

This answer gains the full 12 marks, plus 4 marks for SPaG. It meets AO2, AO3 and AO4 well, and the quality of SPaG is very high.

Practice papers
Set 1

GCSE 9-1 Geography Edexcel B
Practice Paper 1

Global Geographical Issues

Time allowed: 1 hour 30 minutes
Total number of marks: 94 (including 4 marks for spelling, punctuation, grammar and use of specialist terminology (SPaG))

Instructions
Answer **all** questions.

Answer ALL questions. Write your answers in the spaces provided.

Some questions must be answered with a cross in a box ☒. If you change your mind about an answer, put a line through the box ☒ and then mark your new answer with a cross ☒.

1 (a) (i) In which of the following ways do tectonic plates move at a conservative boundary?

(1)

     ☐ **A** Towards one another
     ☒ **B** Side by side
     ☐ **C** Away from each other
     ☐ **D** There is no movement

(ii) At which of the following locations is there an example of a conservative plate boundary?

(1)

     ☐ **A** Iceland
     ☒ **B** California
     ☐ **C** Hawaii
     ☐ **D** Western coast of South America

(b) Explain why the majority of volcanoes and earthquakes occur at plate boundaries.

(2)

This is where Magma can rise from the centre of the earth and cool on the surface to form volcanoes and the movement of two different plate boundaries causes earthquakes - By releasing Pressure

(c) (i) A total of 1482 earthquakes occurred in a seven-day period at the end of April 2016. Calculate the mean number of earthquakes per day, to one decimal place. Show your working.

(2)

0 2 1 1 . 7 1
7) 1 4 8 2 . ⁵0 0

211.7

(ii) Explain why a tsunami is a secondary effect of an earthquake.

(2)

An earthquake causes the ground to move leading to the water being forced upward and the land to be flooded. It is secondary because it occurs after the actual earthquake shock waves causes (tidal waves)

(d) **Figure 2** shows a diagram of the global atmospheric circulation.

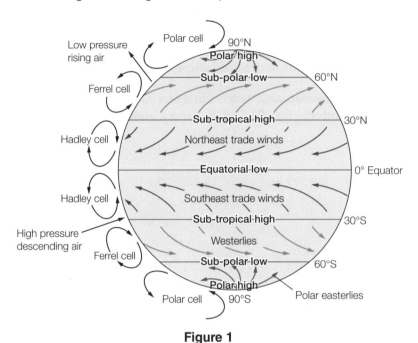

Figure 1

(i) Using **Figure 1**, which **two** of the following statements are true?

(2)

- [ ] **A** Winds blow from low to high pressure.
- [x] **B** High pressure is an area of sinking air.
- [ ] **C** The south-east trades blow in the northern hemisphere.
- [ ] **D** Surface winds are named after the direction that they are blowing towards.
- [x] **E** The UK lies in the westerlies wind belt.
- [ ] **F** Sinking air above the Equator forms the Hadley Cell.

(ii) State **two** effects of the Earth's revolution around the Sun on the pressure and wind belts shown in **Figure 1**.

(2)

1 _____

2 _____

(iii) Explain how the global atmospheric circulation determines the location of the arid regions of the world.

(4)

_____

_____

_____

_____

_____

_____

_____

_____

(e)   **Figure 2** shows changes in Atlantic tropical storms between 1950 and 2010.

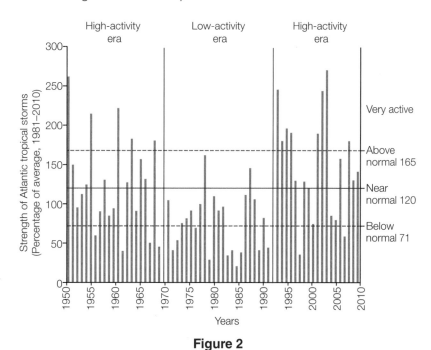

Figure 2

(i)   Identify which **one** of the following data presentation techniques is used in **Figure 2**.

(1)

- ☑ **A**   Bar chart
- ☐ **B**   Pie chart
- ☐ **C**   Line chart
- ☐ **D**   Proportional bar graph

(ii) Suggest **one** reason why there has been an increase in the frequency of strong tropical storms in recent years.

(2)

Climate change has caused more storms and intense rainfall.

(iii) Which of the following is the name given to tropical storms in the Atlantic?

(1)

- ☐ **A**   Cyclones
- ☑ **B**   Hurricanes
- ☐ **C**   Typhoons
- ☐ **D**   Tsunami

(iv) Explain **one** reason why most tropical storms develop between 5° and 15° north and south of the Equator.

(2)

Tropical storms require temperatures above 27°C and this can be found between 5° and 15° north and south of equator. These all large seas here aswell

(f) Evaluate the view that 'the world's developed countries are more effective than developing and emerging countries in their planning and preparation for tropical storms'.

(8)

(Total for Question 1 = 30 marks)
TOTAL FOR SECTION A = 30 MARKS

Section B Development Dynamics

Answer ALL questions. Write your answers in the spaces provided.

2 (a) (i) Identify which of the following statements is a part of Frank's 'dependency theory'.

(1)

☐ **A** A country will go through five stages of development.
☑ **B** The world can be divided into a core and a periphery.
☐ **C** The periphery will export high value goods to the core.
☐ **D** A country's development is not influenced by its history.

(ii) Identify which of the following statements is generally true about a developed country.

(1)

☐ **A** It will have a population pyramid with a wide base.
☐ **B** The Corruption Perception Index will be high.
☑ **C** The literacy rate will be high.
☐ **D** The number of people per doctor will be high.

(b) **Figure 3** shows global variations in HDI.

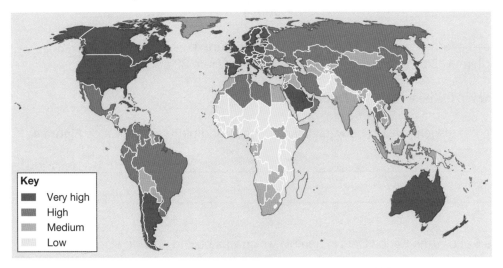

Figure 3

(i) Give the meaning of the letters 'HDI'.

(1)

Human development Index

(ii) Explain **two** advantages of using HDI as a development indicator.

(4)

_____

_____

_____

_____

_____

_____

_____

_____

(c) **Figure 4** is a scattergraph showing the relationship between birth rate and infant mortality rate in a number of countries.

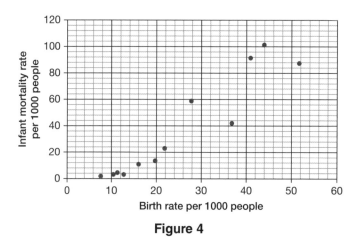

Figure 4

(i) Plot the following data for the Ivory Coast on **Figure 4**.
Birth rate 45 per 1000   Infant mortality rate 82 per 1000

(1)

(ii) Draw in the best fit line on **Figure 4**.

(1)

(iii) Identify the relationship between infant mortality and birth rate shown on **Figure 4**.

(1)

_____

_____

(d) **Figure 5** shows the Kariba Dam in Zambia which was built to provide electricity.

Figure 5

Suggest why dams such as the Kariba Dam are examples of 'top-down' development.

(4)

_____

_____

_____

_____

_____

_____

_____

(e)   **Figure 6** shows an example of intermediate technology used in pumping water.

Figure 6

(i)   Explain why the example shown in **Figure 6** can be considered to be an example of intermediate technology.

(4)

_____

_____

_____

_____

_____

_____

_____

_____

(ii) Explain **one** advantage of intermediate technology as an approach to development.

(2)

_____

_____

_____

_____

(iii) Explain **one** disadvantage of intermediate technology as an approach to development.

(2)

_____

_____

_____

_____

(f) Evaluate the environmental impacts of economic development in a **named** example of an emerging country.

(8)

Name of chosen country: _____

_____

_____

_____

_____

_____

_____

_____

_____

_____

_____

_____

_____

_____

_____

_____

_____

_____

(Total for Question 2 = 30 marks)
TOTAL FOR SECTION B = 30 MARKS

Section C Challenges of an Urbanising World

Answer ALL questions. Write your answer in the spaces provided.

***Spelling, punctuation, grammar and the use of specialist terminology will be assessed in (e).**

3 (a) Identify the correct definition of the term 'urbanisation' from the following.

(1)

☐ **A** Unplanned growth into the surrounding urban area.
☐ **B** When an increasing percentage of a country's population live in towns and cities.
☐ **C** The process by which suburbs grow as a city grows outwards.
☐ **D** The redevelopment of former industrial areas or housing to improve them.

(b) Identify which of the following data presentation techniques could be used to show inequalities between different parts of a city.

(1)

☐ **A** A choropleth map
☐ **B** A flow line map
☐ **C** A line chart
☐ **D** A pie chart

(c) **Figure 7** gives information about the world's megacities.

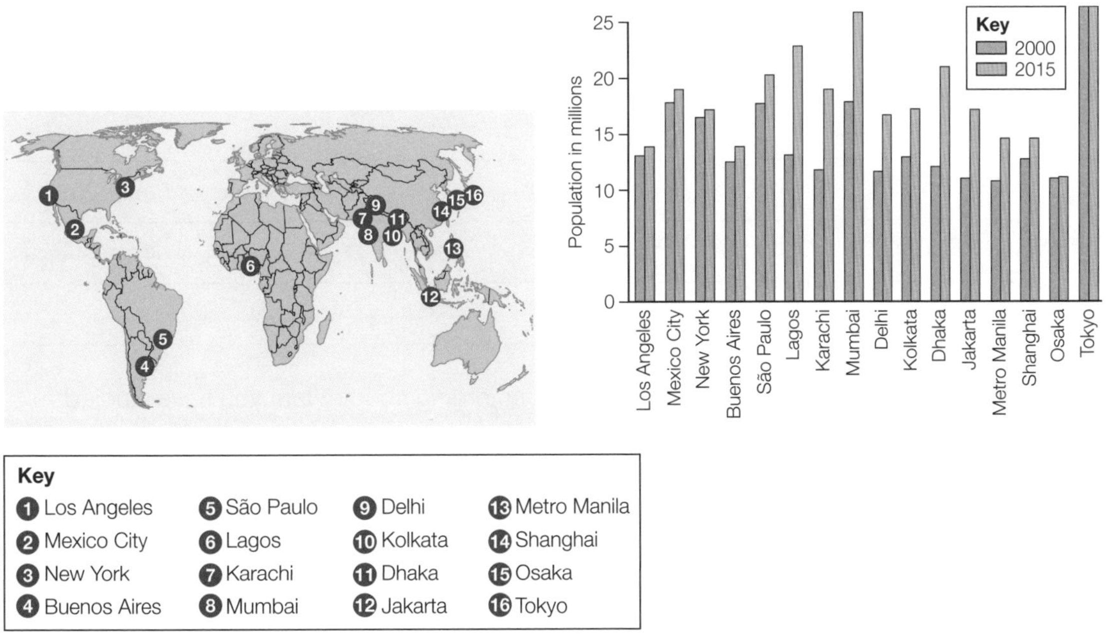
Population in millions
0
5
10
15
20
25
Los Angeles
Mexico City
New York
Buenos Aires
São Paulo
Lagos
Karachi
Mumbai
Delhi
Kolkata
Dhaka
Jakarta
Metro Manila
Shanghai
Osaka
Tokyo
Key
2000
2015
Key
1 Los Angeles
2 Mexico City
3 New York
4 Buenos Aires
5 São Paulo
6 Lagos
7 Karachi
8 Mumbai
9 Delhi
10 Kolkata
11 Dhaka
12 Jakarta
13 Metro Manila
14 Shanghai
15 Osaka
16 Tokyo

Figure 7

(i) Define the term 'megacity'.

(1)

____

____

(ii) Describe the **distribution** of the world's megacities.

(2)

_____

_____

_____

_____

(iii) Compare the **growth** of the world's megacities between 2000 and 2015.

(3)

_____

_____

_____

_____

_____

_____

(iv) Explain why some urban areas can dominate the rest of the country.

(3)

_____

_____

_____

_____

_____

_____

_____

(d) Name a megacity in _either_ a developing _or_ an emerging country that you have studied.

(2)

Name of chosen megacity: _____

(i) Describe the site of your chosen megacity.

_____

_____

_____

_____

(ii) Describe the situation of your chosen megacity.

(2)

_____

_____

_____

_____

(iii) Explain why your chosen megacity has experienced rapid population growth.

(4)

_____

_____

_____

_____

_____

_____

_____

(iv) Describe **one** challenge of living in your chosen megacity that is caused by
its rapid population growth.

(3)

_____

_____

_____

_____

_____

_____

*In this question, 4 of the marks awarded will be for your spelling, punctuation and grammar and your use of specialist terminology

*(e)   Assess the challenges caused by extremes of wealth within your chosen megacity.

(12)

_____

_____

_____

_____

_____

_____

_____

_____

_____

_____

_____

_____

_____

_____

_____

_____

_____

_____

_____

_____

_____

_____

_____

(Total for Question 3 = 34 marks)
TOTAL FOR SECTION C = 34 MARKS
TOTAL FOR THE PAPER = 94 MARKS

GCSE 9-1 Geography Edexcel B
Practice Paper 2

UK Geographical Issues

Time allowed: 1 hour 30 minutes
Total number of marks: 94 (including 4 marks for spelling, punctuation, grammar and use of specialist terminology (SPaG))

Instructions
Answer **all** questions in Section A and Section B
Answer **two** questions in Section C

Answer ALL questions. Write your answers in the spaces provided.

Some questions must be answered with a cross in a box ☒. If you change your mind about an answer, put a line through the box ☒ and mark your new answer with a cross ☒.

***Spelling, punctuation, grammar and the use of specialist terminology will be assessed in question 4.**

1 (a) **Figure 1** shows the distribution of one major rock type found in the British Isles.

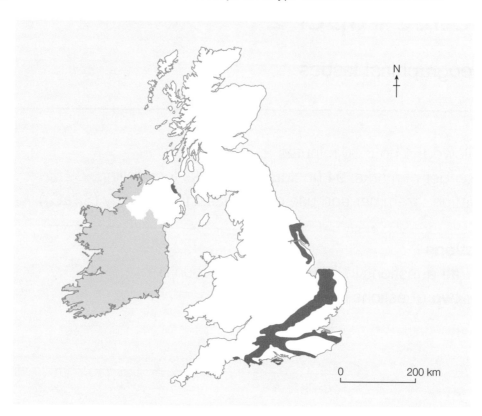

Figure 1

(i) Identify which of the following rock types is found in the areas coloured brown in **Figure 1**.

(1)

☐ **A** Carboniferous limestone
☐ **B** Granite
☐ **C** Sandstone
☐ **D** Chalk

(ii) **Figure 2** shows part of an upland part of the United Kingdom.

Figure 2

This landscape is a typical example of which **one** of the following natural processes?

(1)

☐ **A** Tectonic action
☐ **B** Glacial erosion
☐ **C** Weathering
☐ **D** River erosion

(b) Explain **one** way in which human activity has created distinctive landscapes over time in the UK.

(2)

_____

_____

_____

_____

(Total for Question 1 = 4 marks)

Coastal Change and Conflict

2 (a)   **Figure 3** shows some coastal management techniques.

Figure 3

(i) Identify the coastal management technique labelled **X** in **Figure 3**.

(1)

☐ **A** Beach nourishment
☐ **B** Rock armour
☐ **C** Groyne
☐ **D** Sea wall

(ii) Identify the coastal management technique labelled **Y** in **Figure 3**.

(1)

☐ **A** Beach nourishment
☐ **B** Rock armour
☐ **C** Groyne
☐ **D** Sea wall

(b)　(i)　Using a labelled diagram, explain the process of longshore drift.

(4)

(ii)　Explain **one** reason why people in a coastal area may wish to manage the effects of longshore drift.

(2)

_____

_____

_____

_____

(Total for Question 2 = 8 marks)

River Processes and Pressures

3 (a) Identify which of the following is a description of the river process of attrition.

(1)

☐ **A** The scratching and scraping of a river bed and banks by the stones and sand.
☐ **B** The wearing away of particles by the action of other particles in the river's load.
☐ **C** The velocity of a river.
☐ **D** The dissolving of chemicals by the water in the river.

(b) **Figure 4** shows a storm hydrograph.

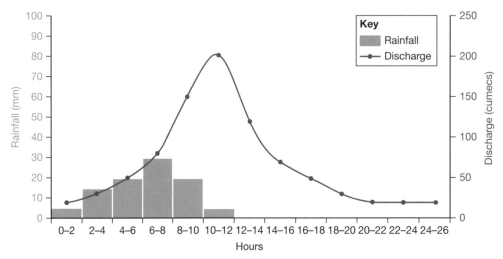

Figure 4

(i) Define the term 'discharge'.

(1)

_____

_____

(ii) Identify the peak discharge in cumecs.

(1)

_____

(iii) Explain how land-use changes can affect the discharge of a river.

(4)

_____

_____

_____

_____

_____

_____

_____

_____

(Total for Question 3 = 7 marks)

Investigating a Geographical Issue

*Spelling, punctuation, grammar and the use of specialist terminology will be assessed in this question.

*4 Figure 5 shows coastal management at Lyme Regis in Dorset.

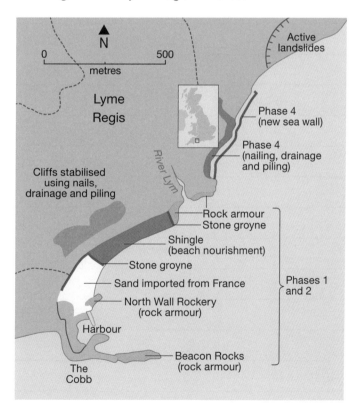

Figure 5

In this question, 4 of the marks awarded will be for your spelling, punctuation and grammar and your use of specialist terminology.

Assess the relative costs and benefits of managing coasts like in **Figure 5** using hard-engineering management strategies.

(12)

_____

_____

_____

_____

_____

_____

_____

_____

_____

_____

_____

_____

_____

_____

_____

_____

_____

_____

_____

_____

(Total for Question 4 = 12 marks)
TOTAL FOR SECTION A = 31 MARKS

Answer ALL questions. Write your answers in the spaces provided.

5 (a) **Figure 6** shows the population structure of the Outer Hebrides 2004–14, an extreme, rural part of the United Kingdom.

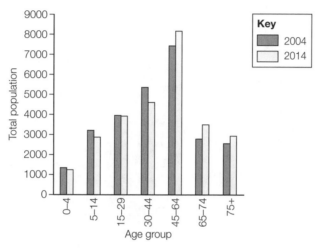

Figure 6

(i) Identify the modal age group in both 2004 and 2014.

(1)

_____

(ii) Suggest one way in which the population structure of the Outer Hebrides could affect economic activity there.

(2)

_____

_____

_____

_____

(iii) Explain **one** attempt to improve the economies of rural areas.

(2)

_____

_____

_____

_____

(Total for Question 5 = 5 marks)

Dynamic UK Cities

6   (a)   **Figure 7** shows part of a city in the UK.

Figure 7

(i)   Identify the part of the city shown in **Figure 7**.

(1)

☐ **A**   CBD
☐ **B**   Inner city
☐ **C**   Suburbs
☐ **D**   Rural–urban fringe

(ii)   Describe **two** features that makes this part of the city distinctive.

(2)

_____

_____

_____

_____

(iii) Explain why areas such as that shown in **Figure 7** may need to be re-branded.

(4)

_____

_____

_____

_____

_____

_____

_____

_____

_____

(b)   **Figure 8** shows a map of the park and ride schemes for the city of Bath in south-west England.

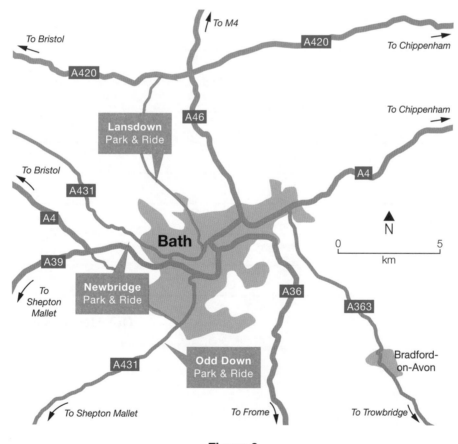

Figure 8

(i) Suggest how these park and ride schemes may affect the city of Bath.

(3)

_____

_____

_____

_____

_____

_____

_____

_____

(ii) Apart from park and ride schemes, explain **two** ways in which people attempt to make urban living more sustainable.

(4)

1 _____

_____

_____

_____

2 _____

_____

_____

_____

(Total for Question 6 = 14 marks)

Investigating a UK Geographical Issue

7 **Figure 9** compares wealth and deprivation in two different parts of the city of Birmingham.

	Sparkbrook	Sutton Four Oaks	Birmingham average
Unemployment (%)	24.5	3.1	12.0
Economically active or at work (%)	48	81	68
Working age population with no qualifications (%)	49.7	20.9	37.1
Pupils with five GCSEs, A*–C (%)	51	74	58
Children living in poverty (%)	49	7	34
Average household income (£)	21 000	40 000	31 000
Households with income less than £15 000 (%)	46	12	27
Households with income over £35 000 (%)	12	47	27

Figure 9

Assess the extent to which there is inequality between different parts of major UK cities, such as Birmingham.

(8)

_____

_____

_____

_____

_____

_____

_____

_____

_____

_____

_____

_____

_____

_____

_____

_____

_____

(Total for Question 7 = 8 marks)
TOTAL FOR SECTION B = 27 MARKS

Section C1 Geographical Investigations: Fieldwork in a Physical Environment

Answer EITHER Question 8 OR Question 9 in this section.
Write your answers in the spaces provided.

If you answer Question 8 put a cross in this box ☐.

Investigating Coastal Change and Conflict

8   You have carried out a fieldwork investigation in a coastal environment.

Name your coastal environment location:

_____

Figure 10 shows some fieldwork equipment that could be used when carrying out a coastal investigation.

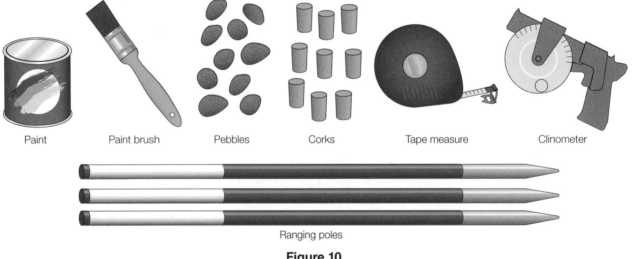

Paint   Paint brush   Pebbles   Corks   Tape measure   Clinometer

Ranging poles

Figure 10

Choose **one** piece of equipment shown in **Figure 10.**

Equipment chosen: _____

(a)   Explain how this equipment can help to collect data at a coastal location from which conclusions can be drawn.

(2)

_____

_____

_____

_____

(b)   **Figure 11** shows a graph of pebble sizes from four samples taken at five locations along a beach.

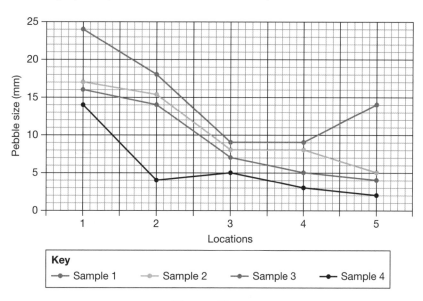

Figure 11

(i)   State **one** reason why this is an inappropriate graph for this type of data.

(1)

_____

_____

(ii) Name a more suitable form of graph to illustrate this type of data.

(1)

_____

_____

(c)   (i)   Explain two challenges that the students might have faced in trying to make their data collection as accurate as possible.

(4)

_____

_____

_____

_____

_____

_____

_____

_____

(ii) Explain one concept or theory that the students who collected data might have been trying to investigate.

(2)

_____

_____

_____

_____

(iii) Evaluate the accuracy and reliability of your conclusions in your coastal fieldwork.

(8)

_____

_____

_____

_____

_____

_____

_____

_____

_____

_____

_____

_____

_____

_____

_____

_____

(Total for Question 8 = 18 marks)

If you answer Question 9 put a cross in this box ☐.

Investigating River Processes and Pressures

9   You have carried out a fieldwork investigation in a river environment.

Name your river environment location:

_____

Figure 12 shows some fieldwork equipment that could be used when carrying out a river investigation.

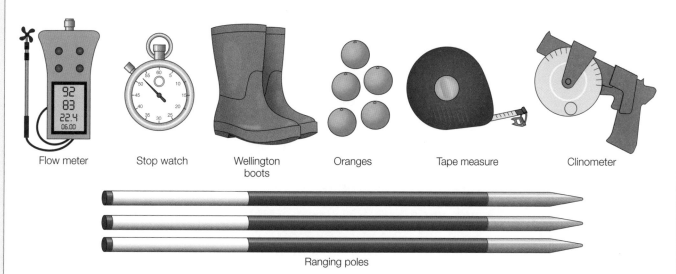

| Flow meter | Stop watch | Wellington boots | Oranges | Tape measure | Clinometer |

Ranging poles

Figure 12

(a)   Choose **one** of the pieces of equipment shown in **Figure 12.**

Equipment chosen: _____

Explain how this equipment can help to collect data at a location on a river from which conclusions can be drawn.

(2)

_____

_____

_____

_____

(b)   **Figure 13** shows a graph of velocity of a river by taking measurements four times at five different locations.

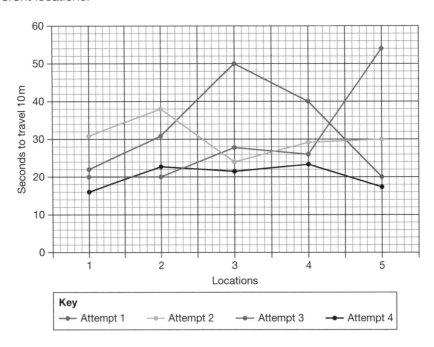

Figure 13

(i)   State one reason why this is an inappropriate graph for this type of data.

(1)

_____

_____

(ii) Name a more suitable form of graph to illustrate this type of data.

(1)

_____

_____

(c)   (i)   Explain two challenges that the students might have faced in trying to make their data collection as accurate as possible.

(4)

_____

_____

_____

_____

_____

_____

_____

_____

(ii) Explain one concept or theory that the students who collected data might have been trying to investigate.

(2)

_____

_____

_____

_____

(iii) Evaluate the accuracy and reliability of your conclusions in your river investigation.

(8)

_____

_____

_____

_____

_____

_____

_____

_____

_____

_____

_____

_____

_____

_____

_____

_____

_____

(Total for Question 9 = 18 marks)
TOTAL FOR SECTION C1 = 18 MARKS

Section C2 Geographical Investigations: Fieldwork in a Human Environment

Answer EITHER Question 10 OR Question 11 in this section.
Write your answers in the spaces provided.

If you answer Question 10 put a cross in this box ☐.

Investigating Dynamic Urban Areas

10 (a)   A group of students investigated people's views on the quality of life in an urban area.

They collected primary data using a questionnaire, choosing a method where they questioned every 10th person that walked past them.

(i)   Identify which **one** type of sampling the students used.

(1)

☐ **A**   Random
☐ **B**   Stratified
☐ **C**   Systematic
☐ **D**   Opportunistic

(ii) The first two questions on the questionnaire required the students to note the age and sex of the person they were questioning.

Explain **one** reason why this information would prove helpful in increasing the accuracy of their findings.

(1)

_____

_____

(b) **Figure 14** shows some secondary information about unemployment, which they included in their write up of their geographical investigation.

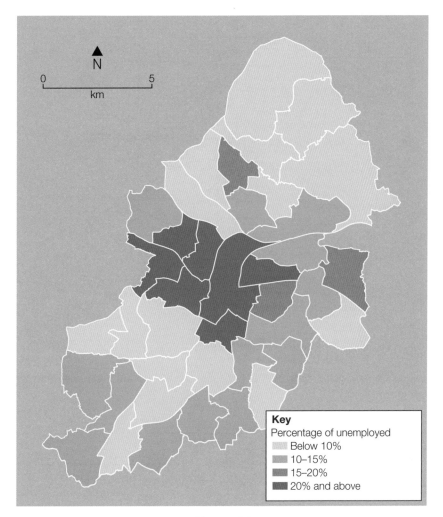

Figure 14

(i) Identify the method of data presentation technique used in **Figure 14**.

(1)

_____

_____

(ii) Explain **one** weakness of this data presentation technique when showing unemployment in an urban area.

(3)

_____

_____

_____

_____

_____

_____

(c)   **Figure 15** is a bi-polar diagram that a student constructed using both primary and secondary data from two different parts of the urban area.

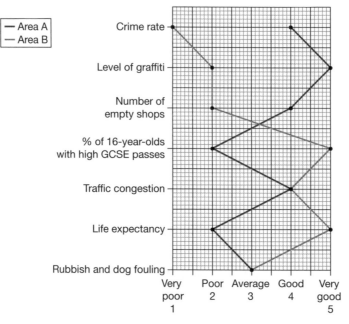

Figure 15

Explain the evidence in **Figure 15** that shows that there are social inequalities in this urban area.

(4)

_____

_____

_____

_____

_____

_____

_____

_____

(d) Evaluate the usefulness of your data collection methods in helping you to investigate variations in urban quality of life.

(8)

_____

_____

_____

_____

_____

_____

_____

_____

_____

_____

_____

_____

_____

_____

_____

_____

_____

_____

(Total for Question 10 = 18 marks)

If you answer Question 11 put a cross in this box ☐.

Investigating Changing Rural Areas

11 A group of students investigated people's views on the quality of life in a rural area.

They collected primary data using a questionnaire, choosing a method where they questioned every 10th person that walked past them.

(a) (i) Identify which **one** type of sampling the students used.

(1)

☐ **A** Random
☐ **B** Stratified
☐ **C** Systematic
☐ **D** Opportunistic

(ii) The first two questions on the questionnaire required the students to note the age and sex of the person they were questioning.

Explain **one** reason why this information would prove helpful in increasing the accuracy of their findings.

(2)

_____

_____

(b)   **Figure 16** shows some secondary information about the provision of services in some Dorset villages, which they included in their write up of their geographical investigation.

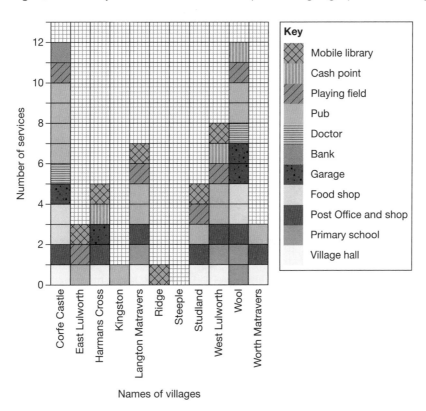

Figure 16

(i)   Identify the data presentation technique used in **Figure 16**.

(1)

_____

_____

(ii)   Explain **one** weakness of this data presentation technique when showing provision of services in a rural area.

(2)

_____

_____

_____

_____

(c) **Figure 17** is bi-polar diagram that a student constructed using data from two different parts of a village in Essex.

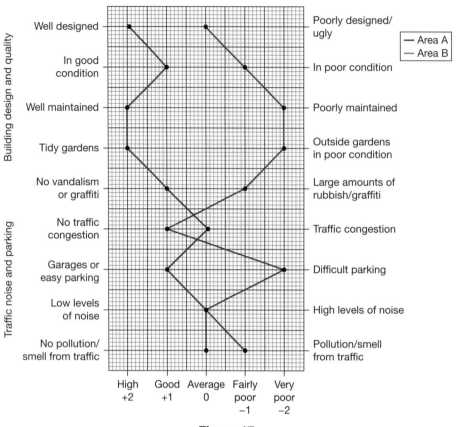

Figure 17

Explain the evidence in **Figure 17** that shows that there are social inequalities in this village.

(4)

_____

_____

_____

_____

_____

_____

_____

_____

(d)   Evaluate the usefulness of your data collection methods in helping you to investigate variations in rural quality of life.

(8)

_____

_____

_____

_____

_____

_____

_____

_____

_____

_____

_____

_____

_____

_____

_____

_____

_____

_____

(Total for Question 11 = 18 marks)
TOTAL FOR SECTION C2 = 18 MARKS
TOTAL FOR PAPER = 94 MARKS

Practice papers
Set 1

GCSE 9-1 Geography Edexcel B
Practice Paper 3

People and Environment Issues –
Making Geographical Decisions

Time allowed: 1 hour 30 minutes
Total number of marks: 64 (including 4 marks for spelling,
punctuation, grammar and use of specialist terminology (SPaG))

Instructions
Answer **all** questions.

Section A People and the Biosphere

Answer ALL questions. Write your answers in the spaces provided.

Some questions must be answered with a cross in a box ☒. If you change your mind about an answer, put a line through the box ☒ and then mark your new answer with a cross ☒.

1   Use Section A in Resource Booklet 1 to answer this question.

(a)   Study **Figure 1**, a map of biomes and **Figure 2**, photographs of five of the biomes shown in **Figure 1**.

Identify the correct letter for each of the biomes. Two have been done for you.

(2)

V	**A**	Desert
	B	Rain Forest
	C	Taiga
X	**D**	Tropical Grassland (Savanna)
	E	Tundra

(b)   Study **Figure 3** in Resource Booklet 1.

Identify which of the following biomes the climate graph represents.

(1)

☐ **A** Desert
☐ **B** Rain Forest
☐ **C** Taiga
☐ **D** Tropical Grassland (Savanna)
☐ **E** Tundra

(c)   Study **Figure 4**, a graph showing biome productivity as measured by biomass, the amount of living material produced in the biome.

(i)   Identify which biome is most productive.

(1)

_____

(ii)   Explain one way in which this biome has resulted from the climate there.

(2)

_____

_____

_____

_____

(d)   Explain how Boserup's theory gives an optimistic view of the balance between population and the availability of food.

(2)

_____

_____

_____

_____

(Total for Question 1 = 8 marks)
TOTAL FOR SECTION A = 8 MARKS

2   Use Section B in Resource Booklet 1 to answer this question.

(a)   **Figure 5** shows the taiga nutrient cycle.

(i)   Name feature **L** on the diagram.

(1)

_____

(ii)   Explain why this feature is the largest in the taiga nutrient cycle.

(2)

_____

_____

_____

_____

(iii)   Explain **one** reason why the taiga has a low level of biodiversity.

(2)

_____

_____

_____

_____

(b)   Complete the following diagram. Join the features of the taiga forest to the reason it is
well adapted to the climate and soil conditions where it grows.
One has been done for you.

(2)

Trees have thick bark	because only the top layer of soil is not frozen permanently.
Trees have needles rather than leaves	to allow snow to slide off easily.
Trees have shallow but widespread roots	to reduce the rate of transpiration.
Trees are conical shaped	to protect trees from very low temperatures.

(Total for Question 2 = 7 marks)
TOTAL FOR SECTION B = 7 MARKS

3 Use Section C in Resource Booklet 1 to answer this question.

(a) **Figures 6A** and **6B** show global patterns of energy consumption and energy supply (production).

Compare the global patterns shown in **Figures 6A** and **6B**.

(3)

_____

_____

_____

_____

_____

_____

(b) **Figure 7** gives information about gas supplies in Europe.

Explain why worsening relations between Russia and Europe could affect Europe's energy security.

(4)

_____

_____

_____

_____

_____

_____

_____

_____

(c) (i) **Figure 8** shows a map of the distribution of the Russian taiga forests.

Identify which one of the following shows the proportion of Russia taken up by taiga.

(1)

☐ **A** 50%   ☐ **B** 60%   ☐ **C** 70%   ☐ **D** 80%

(ii) Study **Figure 9**.

Explain how taiga in Russia may be under threat from commercial interests.

(4)

_____

_____

_____

_____

_____

_____

_____

(d) Study **Figure 10**.

(i) Explain to what extent the distribution of population in Russia reflects the availability of resources shown in **Figure 9**.

(3)

_____

_____

_____

_____

_____

(ii) The population of Russia in 2018 was 144 million.
The estimated population for 2050 is 133 million.

Calculate the projected percentage fall in Russia's population between 2018 and 2050.
Show your working. Give your answer to one decimal point.

(2)

_____

_____

_____

_____

(iii) Using the information in **Figures 10**, **11** and **12**, assess the potential problem for the Russian economy caused by a fall in its population.

(8)

_____

_____

_____

_____

_____

_____

_____

_____

_____

_____

_____

_____

(e) **Figure 13** gives information about Russia's taiga.
Assess the opportunities and challenges faced by developing the Russian taiga.

(8)

_____

_____

_____

_____

_____

_____

_____

_____

_____

_____

_____

_____

Complete your answers on a separate sheet of paper if necessary

(Total for Question 3 = 33 marks)
TOTAL FOR SECTION C = 33 MARKS

*In this question, 4 of the marks will be for your spelling, punctuation and grammar and your use of specialist terminology.

*4 Study these **three** options about how Russia should develop its taiga area of Siberia.

Option 1: Extend the government's policy of encouraging young people to migrate to Siberia.

Option 2: Restrict further commercial development of Siberian taiga by increasing the amount of protected land to 75% of its area, from its present 15%.

Option 3: Encourage local companies and foreign TNCs to invest in Siberia and exploit the resources of the taiga.

Select the option that you think would be the best **long-term** plan for the development of the Russian taiga in Siberia. Justify your choice.

Use information from Resource Booklet 1 and knowledge and understanding from the rest of your geography course to support your answer.

(16)

Chosen option: _____

_____

_____

_____

_____

_____

_____

_____

_____

_____

_____

_____

_____

_____

_____

_____

_____

_____

_____

_____

_____

_____

_____

_____

_____

_____

_____

_____

_____

_____

_____

_____

_____

_____

_____

_____

_____

_____

_____

(Total for Question 4 = 16 marks)
TOTAL FOR SECTION D = 16 MARKS
TOTAL FOR PAPER = 64 MARKS

GCSE 9-1 Geography Edexcel B
Practice Paper 1

Global Geographical Issues

Time allowed: 1 hour 30 minutes
Total number of marks: 94 (including 4 marks for spelling,
punctuation, grammar and use of specialist terminology (SPaG))

Instructions
Answer **all** questions.

Answer ALL questions. Write your answers in the spaces provided

Some questions must be answered with a cross in a box ☒. If you change your mind about an answer, put a line through the box ☒ and mark your new answer with a cross ☒.

***Spelling, punctuation, grammar and the use of specialist terminology will be assessed in 1 (h)**

1 (a)   Name the part of the Earth's structure that is *a hot semi-molten layer that lies beneath the tectonic plates*.

(1)

☐ **A**   Core
☐ **B**   Mantle
☐ **C**   Lithosphere
☐ **D**   Asthenosphere

(b)   Identify which **one** of the following is **not** a feature of the global atmospheric circulation.

(1)

☐ **A**   There is high pressure at the Poles.
☐ **B**   There is a hot wet climate where the Hadley Cells meet.
☐ **C**   There a hot wet climate where the Hadley and Ferrel Cells meet.
☐ **D**   There is unsettled weather at 60°N and S where the Polar and Ferrel Cells meet.

(c)   (i)   Explain **one** way in which tectonic plates move.

(2)

_____

_____

_____

(ii) Explain the processes that take place at a convergent plate boundary.

(4)

_____

_____

_____

_____

_____

_____

_____

_____

(d)   State **two** conditions necessary for the formation of a tropical storm.

(2)

1 _____

2 _____

(e)   **Figure 1** shows a cross section through a tropical storm

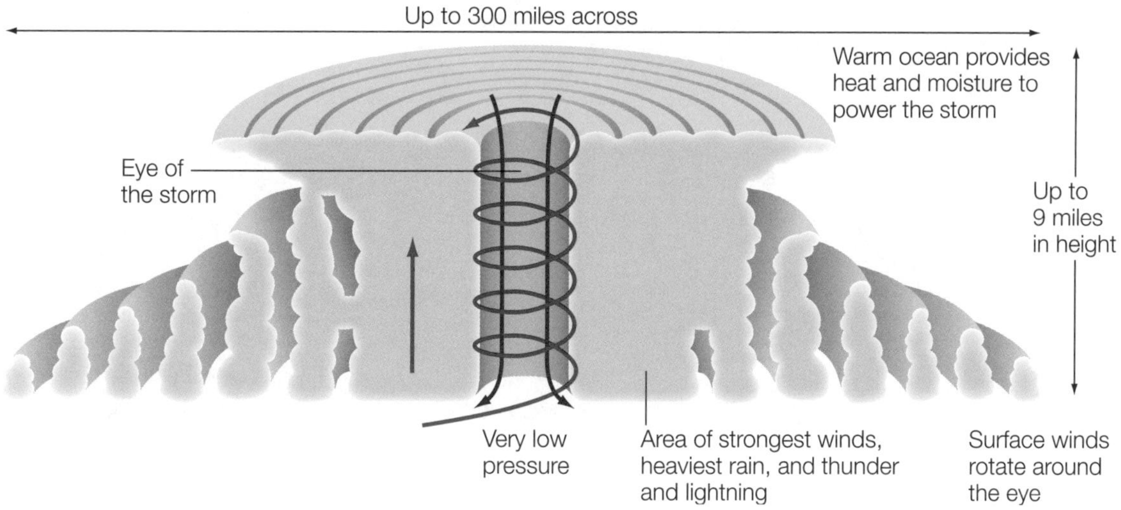

Up to 300 miles across

Warm ocean provides
heat and moisture to
power the storm

Eye of
the storm

Up to
9 miles
in height

Very low
pressure

Area of strongest winds,
heaviest rain, and thunder
and lightning

Surface winds
rotate around
the eye

Figure 1

Using **Figure 1** and your own knowledge, explain: (4)

1   why tropical storms bring heavy rain

_____

_____

_____

_____

2   why tropical storms bring very high winds.

_____

_____

_____

_____

(f)   **Figure 2** shows the effects of a tropical storm.

Figure 2

Name **two** *primary* and **two** *secondary* effects of a tropical storm.

(4)

Primary

1 _____

2 _____

Secondary

1 _____

2 _____

(g)   Explain **two** natural causes of climate change.

(4)

1 _____

_____

_____

_____

2 _____

_____

_____

_____

_____

*In this question, 4 of the marks awarded will be for your spelling, punctuation and grammar and your use of specialist terminology

*(h)   **Figure 3** shows areas of the world threatened by climate change.

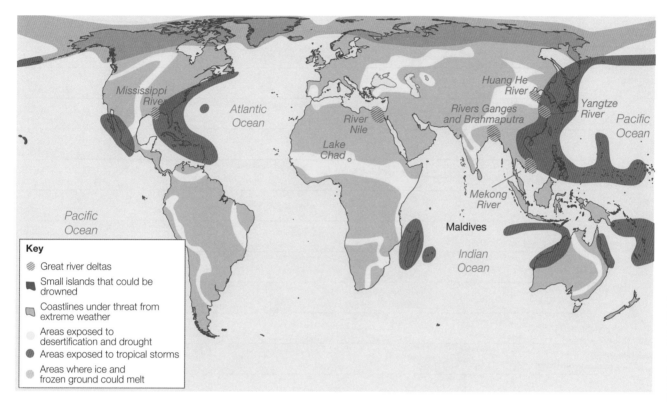

Figure 3

Evaluate the potential effects of climate change on people and the environment.   (12)

_____

_____

_____

_____

_____

_____

_____

_____

_____

_____

_____

_____

(lined answer space)

(Total for Question 1 = 34 marks)
TOTAL FOR SECTION A = 34 MARKS

Answer ALL questions. Write your answers in the spaces provided

2 (a) (i) Define the term 'fertility rate'.

(1)

_____

_____

(ii) Study the following development indicators for three countries **X**, **Y** and **Z**.

Country	GDP per head (US$)	HDI	Birth rate (per 1000 per year)	Death Rate (per 1000 per year)	Infant mortality (per 1000 live births per year)	Maternal mortality (per 100 000 live births)	Fertility rate	Index of Political corruption (maximum 100)
X	15 500	0.755	14.46	6.58	18.60	44	1.75	40
Y	59 500	0.915	12.49	9.35	5.87	14	1.87	74
Z	2300	0.509	32.26	10.13	26.11	443	3.98	22

Figure 4

Using letters **X, Y** or **Z**, identify each country below by the development indicators in **Figure 4**.

(2)

[ ] A developed country

[ ] A developing country

[ ] An emerging country

(b)   **Figures 5** and **6** give details about the African country of Burkina Faso.

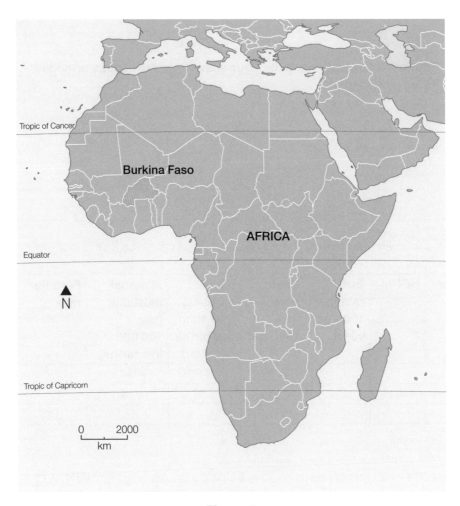

Tropic of Cancer

Burkina Faso

AFRICA

Equator

N

Tropic of Capricorn

0   2000
km

Figure 5

Burkina Faso fact file

- GNI (world ranking 164/188)
- HDI (world ranking 185/188)
- Surrounded by six countries
- Receives about 600–900 mm of rain per year
- Rainy season of four months or less
- Current environmental issues include: recent droughts and desertification severely affecting agricultural activities, overgrazing, soil degradation
- 80% employed in agriculture
- 48% unemployment rate
- Succession of governments overthrown by force since gaining independence from France

Figure 6

Explain **one** physical cause and **one** human cause of Burkina Faso's low level of development.

(4)

Physical causes: _____

_____

_____

_____

Human causes: _____

_____

_____

_____

(c)   Suggest how Burkina Faso's location in Africa may be an obstacle to its development.

(2)

_____

_____

_____

_____

(d)   Explain how TNCs may help to reduce the development gap between countries like Burkina Faso and more developed parts of the world.

(4)

_____

_____

_____

_____

_____

_____

_____

_____

_____

(e) **Figure 7** shows how employment has changed in an emerging country between 1991 and 2017.

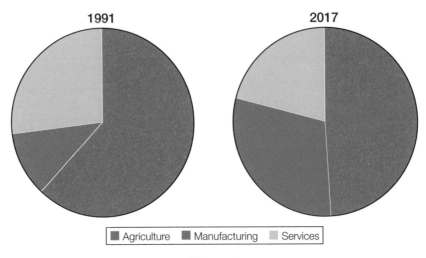

Figure 7

Identify the evidence in **Figure 7** that shows this country had become an emerging country by 2017.

(1)

_____

_____

(f) **Figure 8** shows rubbish dumped on the roadside in an emerging country.

Figure 8

(i) Explain why waste dumps such as this may be common in emerging countries.

(4)

_____

_____

_____

_____

_____

_____

_____

_____

(ii) Explain how economic growth in an emerging country can have **other** harmful impacts
on the environment.

(4)

_____

_____

_____

_____

_____

_____

(g) Evaluate the extent to which manufacturing has increased the level of economic development
in a named emerging country.

(8)

Name of emerging country: _____

_____

_____

_____

_____

_____

_____

_____

_____

_____

_____

_____

_____

_____

_____

_____

_Complete your answer on a separate sheet of paper
if necessary_

(Total for Question 2 = 30 marks)
TOTAL FOR SECTION B = 30 MARKS

Answer ALL questions. Write your answer in the spaces provided

3 (a) (i) Identify which of the following statements is a correct description of a CBD.

(1)

☐ **A** It is a largely residential area.
☐ **B** Its main function is industrial.
☐ **C** It contains a high percentage of shops and offices.
☐ **D** It is the least accessible part of the city.

(ii) **Figure 9** shows how the global urban population is estimated to change by 2050.

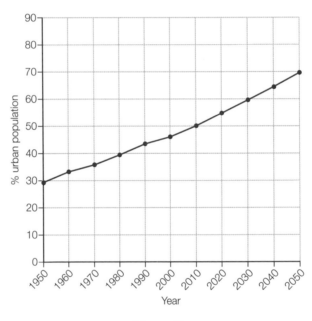

Figure 9

Identify the percentage increase of the world's urban population between 1950 and 2050.

(1)

☐ **A** 30
☐ **B** 40
☐ **C** 50
☐ **D** 60

(b) **Figure 10** shows the growth of cities in Africa, 2010–2015.

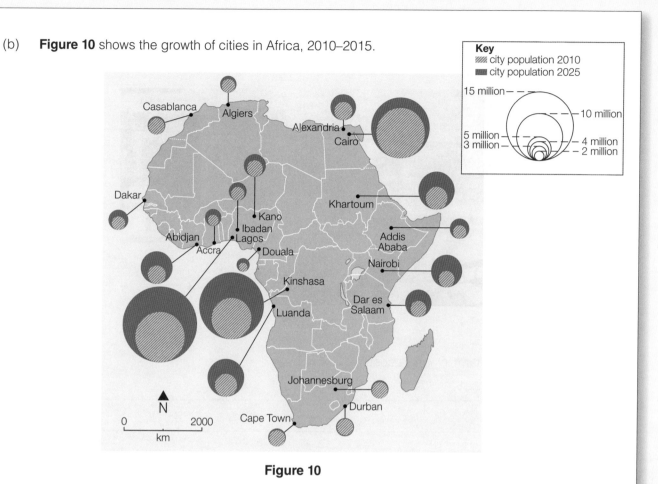

Figure 10

(i) Identify and name the largest city in Africa in 2025.

(1)

_____

(ii) Identify the increase in the population of Cairo between 2010 and 2025.

(1)

_____

(iii) Identify which African city will have the greatest population increase between 2010 and 2025.

(1)

_____

(iv) Explain why a growing percentage of Africans live in urban areas.

(4)

_____

_____

_____

_____

_____

_____

_____

_____

(c)   **Figure 11** shows a street vendor in one of the world's megacities, an example of
        the informal economy.

Figure 11

(i) Define the term informal economy.

(1)

_____

_____

(ii) Explain why the informal economy is important to cities in both developing and
     emerging countries.

(2)

_____

_____

_____

_____

(iii) Explain **two** disadvantages of the informal economy to people who work in it.

(4)

_____

_____

_____

_____

_____

_____

_____

_____

(d)   Name **one** megacity you have studied in a developing or emerging country.

_____

(i) **Figure 12** is a model of the structure of a city in a developing or emerging country.

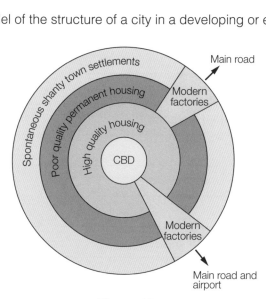

Figure 12

Identify **one** similarity and **one** difference between the model in **Figure 12** and your chosen megacity

Similarity
                                                                                                    (2)
_____

_____

Difference

_____

_____

(ii) Explain how recent growth of your chosen megacity has affected its land-use pattern.
                                                                                                    (4)
_____

_____

_____

_____

_____

_____

_____

_____

(iii) Evaluate the success of **one** top-down strategy which aims to make your chosen megacity more sustainable.

(8)

_____

_____

_____

_____

_____

_____

_____

_____

_____

_____

_____

_____

_____

_____

_____

(Total for Question 3 = 30 marks)
TOTAL FOR SECTION C = 30 MARKS
TOTAL FOR THE PAPER = 94 MARKS

GCSE 9-1 Geography Edexcel B
Practice Paper 2

UK Geographical Issues

Time allowed: 1 hour 30 minutes
Total number of marks: 94 (including 4 marks for spelling,
punctuation, grammar and use of specialist terminology (SPaG))

Instructions
Answer **all** questions in Section A and Section B
Answer **two** questions in Section C

Answer ALL questions. Write your answers in the spaces provided

Some questions must be answered with a cross in a box ☒. If you change your mind about an answer, put a line through the box ☒ and mark your new answer with a cross ☒.

1 (a)   **Figure 1** shows a lowland area of southern England.

Figure 1

(i)   Identify which **one** of the following has played a role in the development of this landscape.

(1)

☐ **A**   Current tectonic activity
☐ **B**   The geology of chalk and clay
☐ **C**   Glacial erosion and deposition
☐ **D**   Freeze-thaw weathering

(ii)   Describe **one** human activity that has influenced the distinctive features of this landscape.

(3)

_____

_____

_____

_____

_____

_____

(Total for Question 1 = 4 marks)

Coastal Change and Conflict

2 **Figure 2** shows several coastal landforms.

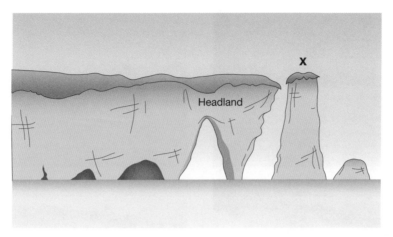

Figure 2

(a) (i) Identify the landform at **X** from the following:

(1)

☐ **A** Cliff   ☐ **B** Spit   ☐ **C** Stack   ☐ **D** Wave-cut platform

(ii) Explain **two** processes that have led to the formation of the landform at **X**.

(4)

_____

_____

_____

_____

_____

_____

_____

_____

(b) Compare the meaning of the terms 'destructive waves' and 'constructive waves'.

(3)

_____

_____

_____

_____

_____

(Total for Question 2 = 8 marks)

River Processes and Pressures

3 (a) **Figure 3** shows four different forms of river management strategies.

Figure 3

Write the correct letter (**W**, **X**, **Y**, **Z**) against each example of a flood management strategy.

(3)

☐ **A** Flood Barrier   ☐ **C** River Restoration

☐ **B** Flood Relief Channel   ☐ **D** Floodwall

(b) Explain why soft engineering is considered to be more acceptable than hard engineering as a flood control management strategy.

(4)

_____

_____

_____

_____

_____

_____

_____

_____

(Total for Question 3 = 7 marks)

Investigating a UK Geographical Issue

4 **Figure 4** shows part of the north coast of Cornwall.

Figure 4

Evaluate the impact of geology and the physical processes on the formation of distinctive coastal landscapes such as that shown in **Figure 4**.

(8)

_____

_____

_____

_____

_____

_____

_____

_____

_____

_____

_____

_____

_____

_____

_____

_____

(Total for Question 4 = 8 marks)
TOTAL FOR SECTION A = 27 MARKS

Answer ALL questions. Write your answer in the spaces provided.

5 (a) **Figure 5** shows changes in UK employment 1984–2014.

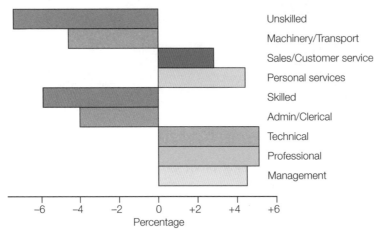

Figure 5

(i) Describe the employment trends shown on **Figure 5**.

(2)

_____

_____

_____

_____

(ii) Explain **one** reason for these trends during this period.

(3)

_____

_____

_____

_____

_____

_____

(Total for Question 5 = 5 marks)

Dynamic UK Cities

6 (a) **Figure 6** shows the distance to essential services for people living in a rural village.

Services	Distance (miles)
Primary School	4
Pub	6
Doctor/pharmacy	7
General store	11
Clothes shop	15
Bank	21
Supermarket	21

Figure 6

(i) Explain how quality of life in this village may be affected by these distances.

(4)

_____

_____

_____

_____

_____

_____

_____

_____

(ii) Explain how new economic opportunities may help overcome the challenges of living in a remote rural area.

(4)

_____

_____

_____

_____

_____

_____

_____

_____

(b)   **Figure 7** shows part of an old industrial area in the city of Bristol that has undergone regeneration.

Figure 7

(i) Identify **two** pieces of evidence from **Figure 7** that suggest the area has been regenerated.

(2)

1_____

2 _____

(ii) Explain how the regeneration of **one** named major UK city has had positive impacts on people.

(4)

Name of major UK city: _____

_____

_____

_____

_____

_____

_____

_____

_____

_____

_____

(Total for Question 6 = 14 marks)

Investigating a UK Geographical Issue

*Spelling, punctuation, grammar and use of specialist terminology will be assessed in this question.

*7 Figure 8 shows the impact of international migration on Great Britain.

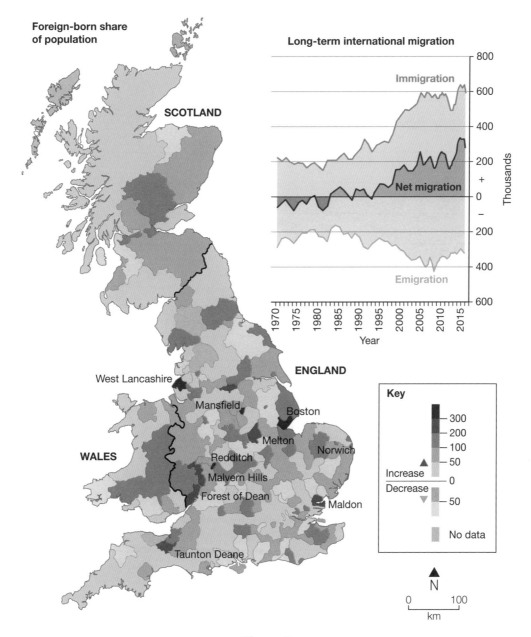

Figure 8

*In this question, 4 of the marks awarded will be for your spelling, punctuation and grammar and your use of specialist terminology

Assess the impacts of international migration over the last 50 years on the population geography of Great Britain.

(12)

_____

_____

_____

_____

_____

_____

_____

_____

_____

_____

_____

_____

_____

_____

_____

_____

_____

_____

_____

_____

_____

_____

_____

(Total for Question 7 = 12 marks)
TOTAL FOR SECTION B = 31 MARKS

Section C1 Geographical Investigation: Fieldwork in a Physical Environment

Answer EITHER Question 8 OR Question 9 in this section.
Write your answers in the spaces provided

If you answer Question 8 put a cross in this box ☐.

Investigating Coastal Change and Conflict

8 (a) For their GCSE fieldwork, a student investigated changes in pebble size along a beach. **Figure 9** shows the results from 12 locations.

Location	Pebble size (mm)
1	12
2	14
3	2
4	6
5	2
6	42
7	12
8	4
9	4
10	18
11	2
12	2

Figure 9

(i) The student worked out the mean, median and the mode to show the central tendency. Write the word *mean, median* or *mode* against the correct figure in the following table.

(2)

Measure of central tendency	
	2
	10
	5

(ii) Explain why the mean value may not be a reliable indicator of pebble size.

(2)

____

____

____

____

(b) **Figure 10** is a dispersion graph which uses the data from **Figure 9**.

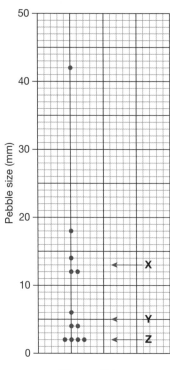

Figure 10

(i) Three values are labelled **X**, **Y** and **Z**.
Complete the following table by writing the correct letter against the appropriate value.

(2)

Name	Letter
Lower Quartile	
Upper Quartile	

(ii) Calculate the interquartile range. Show your working.

(2)

_____

_____

_____

_____

(iii) Explain how the interquartile range can be a useful statistical technique when analysing fieldwork data.

(2)

_____

_____

_____

_____

(c)   You have carried out a fieldwork investigation in a coastal environment.
      State the question or hypothesis that you used for your investigation.

      Question or hypothesis _____

      _____

      Evaluate the reliability of your conclusions in your coastal fieldwork investigation.

      (8)

      _____

      _____

      _____

      _____

      _____

      _____

      _____

      _____

      _____

      _____

      _____

      _____

      _____

      _____

      _____

      _____

      (Total for Question 8 = 18 marks)

If you answer Question 9 put a cross in this box ☐.

Investigating River Processes and Pressures

9 (a) For their GCSE fieldwork, a student investigated changes in pebble size at locations along a river.
Figure 11 shows the results from ten locations.

Location	Pebble size (mm)
1	22
2	19
3	21
4	13
5	7
6	9
7	7
8	7
9	13
10	2

Figure 11

(i) The student worked out the mean, median and the mode from these figures to show the central tendency.
Write the word *mean, median* or *mode* against the correct figure in the following table.

(2)

Measure of central tendency	
	7
	12
	11

(ii) Explain why the mean value of the data shown in **Figure 11** may not be a reliable indicator of pebble size.

(2)

_____

_____

_____

_____

(b) **Figure 12** is a dispersion graph which uses the figures from **Figure 11**.

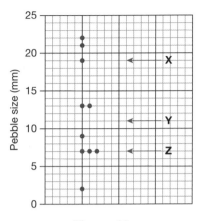

Figure 12

(i) Three values are labelled **X**, **Y** and **Z**.
Complete the following table by writing the correct letter against the appropriate value.

(2)

Name	Letter
Lower Quartile	
Upper Quartile	

(ii) Calculate the interquartile range. Show your working.

(2)

_____

_____

_____

_____

(iii) Explain how the interquartile range can be a useful statistical technique when analysing fieldwork data.

(2)

_____

_____

_____

_____

(c)   You have carried out a fieldwork investigation on a river
       State the question or hypothesis that you used as a title for your investigation.

       Question or hypothesis _____

       _____

       Evaluate the reliability of your conclusions in your river fieldwork investigation

                                                                                   (8)

       _____

       _____

       _____

       _____

       _____

       _____

       _____

       _____

       _____

       _____

       _____

       _____

       _____

       _____

       _____

       _____

       _____

                                              (Total for Question 9 = 18 marks)
                                              TOTAL FOR SECTION C1 = 18 MARKS

Answer EITHER Question 10 OR Question 11 in this section.
Write your answers in the spaces provided

If you answer Question 10 put a cross in this box ☐.

Investigating Dynamic Urban Areas

10   (a) The graphs in **Figure 13** below show published data about different areas of Bristol.

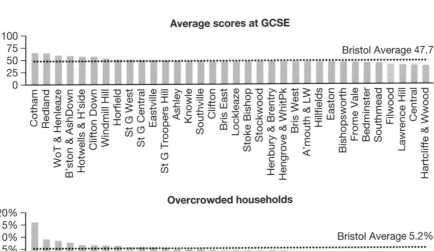

Average scores at GCSE

Bristol Average 47.7

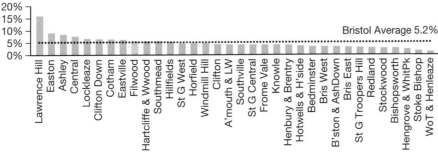

Overcrowded households

Bristol Average 5.2%

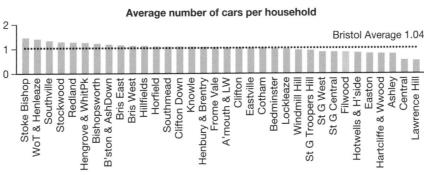

Average number of cars per household

Bristol Average 1.04

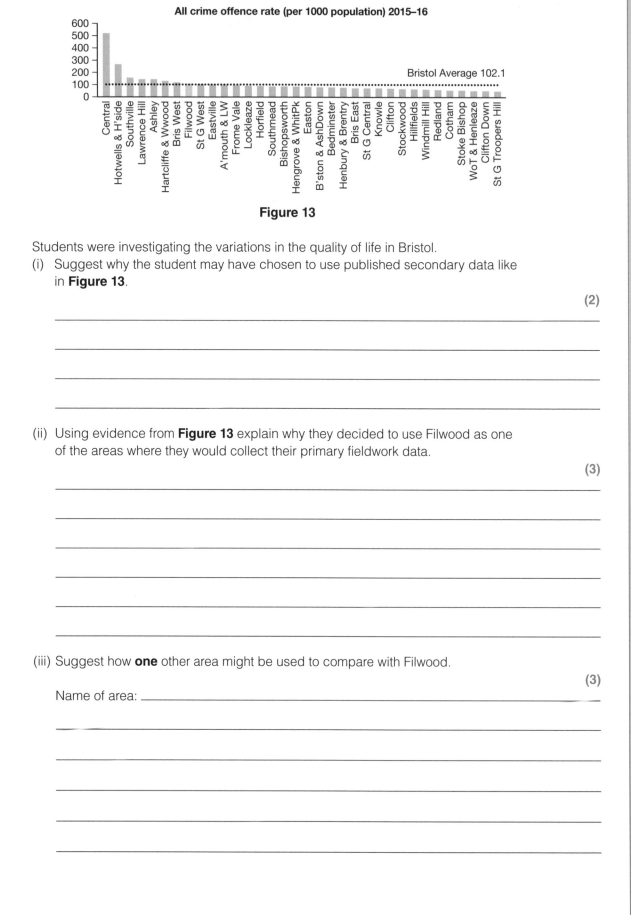

Figure 13

Students were investigating the variations in the quality of life in Bristol.

(i) Suggest why the student may have chosen to use published secondary data like in **Figure 13**.

(2)

_____

_____

_____

_____

(ii) Using evidence from **Figure 13** explain why they decided to use Filwood as one of the areas where they would collect their primary fieldwork data.

(3)

_____

_____

_____

_____

_____

_____

(iii) Suggest how **one** other area might be used to compare with Filwood.

(3)

Name of area: _____

_____

_____

_____

_____

_____

(b)   You have undertaken your own fieldwork investigating variations in the quality of life within an urban area

Name your urban environment fieldwork location. _____

Name **one** set of data you collected. _____

(i)   Explain why the method of data presentation you used to illustrate this set of data helped with its interpretation.

(2)

_____

_____

_____

_____

(ii) Evaluate the extent to which your primary data supported other secondary data that you used in the investigation.

(8)

_____

_____

_____

_____

_____

_____

_____

_____

_____

_____

_____

_____

_____

_____

_____

_____

(Total for Question 10 = 18 marks)

If you answer Question 11 put a cross in this box ☐.

Investigating Changing Rural Areas

11 (a) The graphs in **Figure 14** show published data about five villages in a rural part of England.

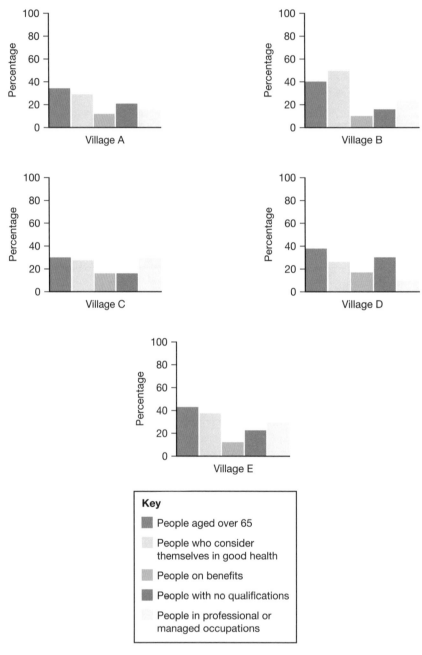

Figure 14

Students were investigating deprivation in a rural area.

(i) Suggest why the student may have chosen to use published secondary data like in **Figure 14**.

(2)

_____

_____

_____

_____

(ii) Using evidence from **Figure 14** explain why they decided to use village D as one of the villages where they would collect their primary fieldwork data.

(3)

_____

_____

_____

_____

_____

_____

(iii) Suggest how **one** other village might be used to compare with village D.

(3)

Letter of village: _____   _____

_____

_____

_____

_____

(b) You have undertaken your own fieldwork investigating variations in the quality of life within a rural area.

Name your rural environment fieldwork location. _____

Name **one** set of data you collected. _____

(i) Explain why the method of data presentation you used to illustrate this set of data helped with its interpretation.

(2)

_____

_____

_____

_____

(ii) Evaluate the extent to which your primary data supported other secondary data that you used in the investigation.

(8)

_____

_____

_____

_____

_____

_____

_____

_____

_____

_____

_____

_____

_____

_____

_____

(Total for Question 11 = 18 marks)
TOTAL FOR SECTION C2 = 18 MARKS
TOTAL FOR PAPER = 94 MARKS

Practice papers
Set 2

GCSE 9-1 Geography Edexcel B
Practice Paper 3

People and Environment Issues –
Making Geographical Decisions

Time allowed: 1 hour 30 minutes
Total number of marks: 64 (including 4 marks for spelling,
punctuation, grammar and use of specialist terminology (SPaG))

Instructions
Answer **all** questions.

Answer ALL questions. Write your answers in the spaces provided

Some questions must be answered with a cross in a box ☒. If you change your mind about an answer, put a line through the box ☒ and then mark you new answer with a cross

1   Use Section A in Resource Booklet 2 to answer these questions.

(a)   (i)   Identify which of the following is **not** a factor that can alter a global biome **locally**.

(1)

☐ **A** Latitude
☐ **B** Soil type
☐ **C** Drainage
☐ **D** Rock type

(ii) **Figure 1** shows an example of a small-scale ecosystem.
Name **one** abiotic and **one** biotic component shown on **Figure 1**.

(2)

Abiotic _____   Biotic _____

(iii) Explain how **one** local factor has altered the characteristics of the global biome
at this location.

(2)

_____

_____

_____

_____

(b)   **Figures 2** and **3** show global population growth in 2015 and the global distribution
of biomes.

(i) Identify which continent shows the greatest rate of population growth.

(1)

_____

(ii) Identify the **two** biomes likely to be most affected by this high growth rate.

(2)

1 _____

2 _____

(Total for Question 1 = 8 marks)
TOTAL FOR SECTION A = 8 MARKS

2 Use Section B in Resource Booklet 2 to answer these questions.

(a) **Figure 4** shows a vegetation map of the Democratic Republic of the Congo (DRC), a country in Africa. Identify **one** piece of evidence in **Figure 4** that the area covered by tropical rainforest was once larger.

(1)

_____

(b) Identify **two** features of the climate of the DRC that allow tropical rainforests to grow there.

(2)

1 _____

2 _____

(c) Study **Figures 5** and **6**. Suggest why the loss of forest cover in the DRC is important for the country as well as globally.

(4)

Importance for the DRC: _____

_____

_____

Importance globally: _____

_____

_____

(d) Study **Figures 7**, **8**, **9** and **10**.
Explain how the changing population of the DRC could explain changes in crop production between 2010 and 2030.

(4)

_____

_____

_____

_____

_____

_____

_____

_____

(Total for Question 2 = 11 marks)
TOTAL FOR SECTION B = 11 MARKS

3 Use Section C in Resource Booklet 2 to answer these questions.

(a) Study **Figure 11**, which gives information about the way of life of the indigenous people of the rainforest.
Explain why the way of life of the indigenous people can be considered sustainable use of the rainforest.

(4)

_____

_____

_____

_____

_____

_____

_____

(b) Study **Figure 12**. 98% of the population of the DRC use firewood as their source of energy in their homes.
Explain why, **apart from deforestation**, the following two factors are important because of the over-reliance on the use of firewood.

(4)

Impact on people's health: _____

_____

_____

Impact on woman's place in society: _____

_____

_____

(c) (i) Give one reason why, in a developing country like the DRC, the demand for energy will constantly be increasing.

(1)

_____

_____

_____

(ii) **Figure 13** shows the cost and benefits of developing HEP as a source of energy
in the DRC.
Assess the suitability of developing HEP in the DRC.

(8)

_____

_____

_____

_____

_____

_____

_____

_____

_____

_____

_____

_____

_____

_____

_____

(iii) Study **Figure 14**, a photograph of Inga 1 and 2 HEP installations on the Congo River.
Suggest **two** impacts of the construction of these HEP installations on the environment
of the rainforest.

(4)

_____

_____

_____

_____

_____

_____

_____

(iv) **Figure 15** gives information about the proposed Inga 3 HEP project.
Assess why there is such a range of views about building this project.

(8)

_____

_____

_____

_____

_____

_____

_____

_____

_____

_____

_____

_____

_____

_____

_____

_____

(Total for Question 3 = 29 marks)
TOTAL FOR SECTION C = 29 MARKS

*In this question, 4 of the marks awarded will be for your spelling, punctuation and grammar and your use of specialist terminology.

*4 Study the **three** options below for how the DRC should provide sufficient energy to provide for its population and form the basis of the development of the country in the 21st century.

> **Option 1**: Build fewer large-scale, top-down, capital-intensive energy generating schemes and encourage more small-scale, bottom-up projects.

> **Option 2**: Adopt more sustainable management of the DRC's rainforests including replanting to replace deforestation caused by building energy installations.

> **Option 3**: Expand large-scale HEP generation as the only practical way of solving the DRC's energy needs.

Select the option that would be the best plan to ensure **long-term** energy security for the DRC, and the environment.

Use information from Resource Booklet 2, and knowledge and understanding from the rest of your geography course to support your answer.

(16)

Chosen option: _____

_____

_____

_____

_____

_____

_____

_____

_____

_____

_____

_____

_____

_____

_____

_____
_____
_____
_____
_____
_____
_____
_____
_____
_____
_____
_____
_____
_____
_____
_____
_____
_____
_____
_____
_____
_____
_____
_____
_____
_____

(Total for Question 4 = 16 marks)
TOTAL FOR SECTION D = 16 MARKS
TOTAL FOR PAPER = 64 MARKS

Figure 1

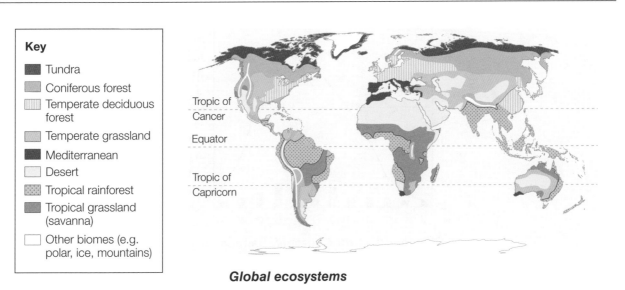

Key

- ■ Tundra
- ▦ Coniferous forest
- ▥ Temperate deciduous forest
- ▨ Temperate grassland
- ■ Mediterranean
- □ Desert
- ▦ Tropical rainforest
- ▦ Tropical grassland (savanna)
- □ Other biomes (e.g. polar, ice, mountains)

Tropic of Cancer

Equator

Tropic of Capricorn

Global ecosystems

Figure 2

V

W

X

Y

Z

Figure 3

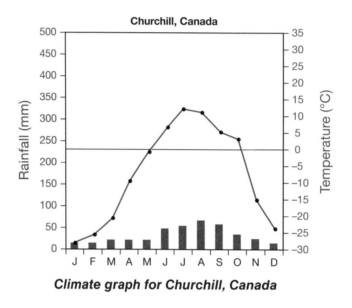

Climate graph for Churchill, Canada

Figure 4

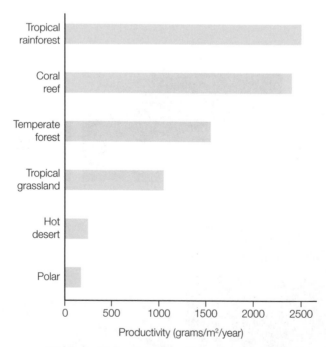

Biome productivity measured by biomass

Figure 5

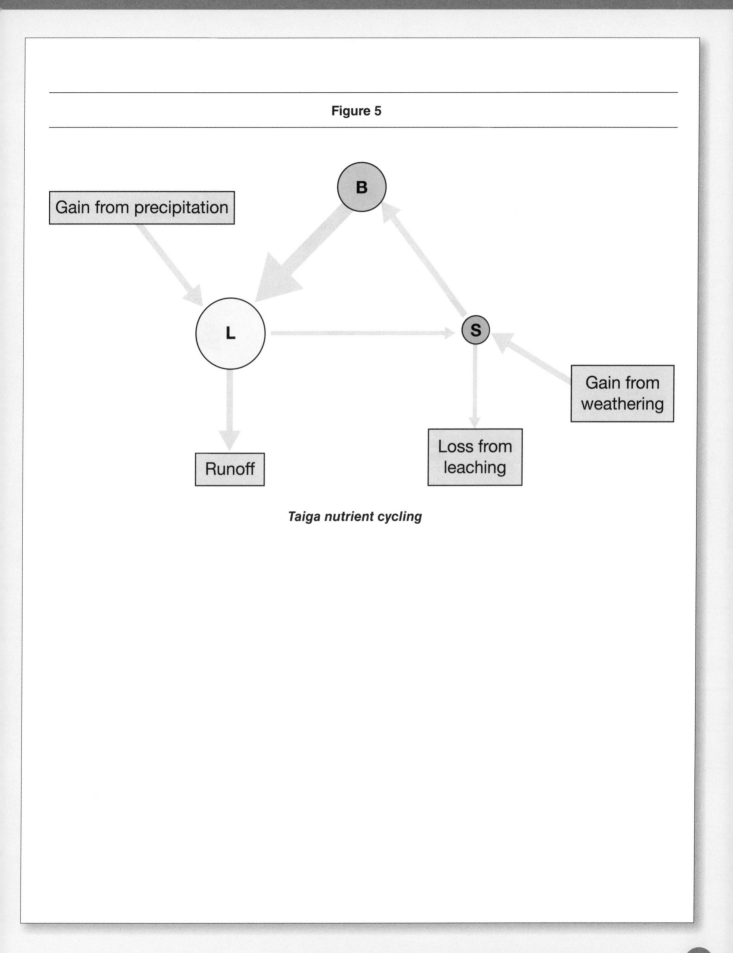

Gain from precipitation

B

L

S

Gain from weathering

Runoff

Loss from leaching

Taiga nutrient cycling

Section C Consuming Energy Resources

Figure 6

A

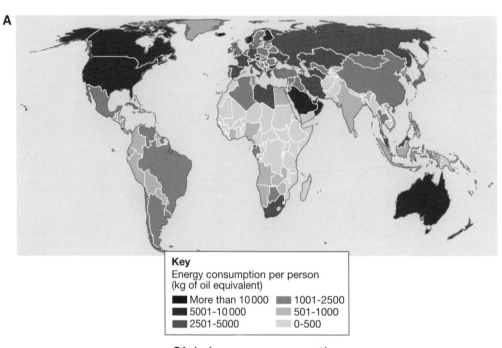

Key

Energy consumption per person
(kg of oil equivalent)

- More than 10 000
- 5001-10 000
- 2501-5000
- 1001-2500
- 501-1000
- 0-500

Global energy consumption

B

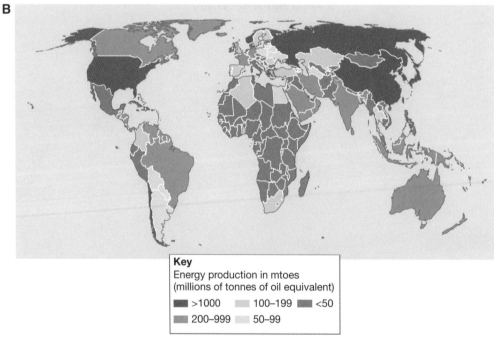

Key

Energy production in mtoes
(millions of tonnes of oil equivalent)

- >1000
- 200–999
- 100–199
- 50–99
- <50

Global energy production

Figure 7

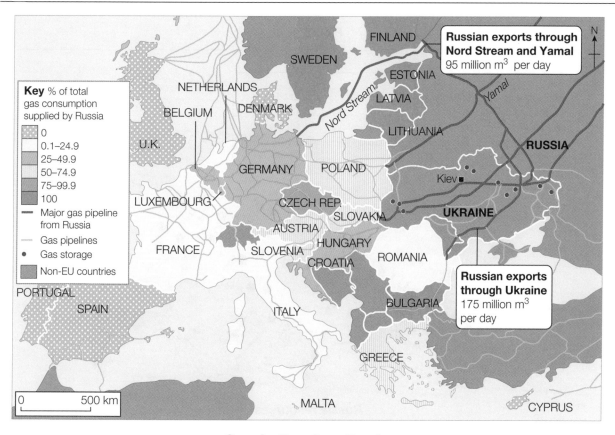

Key % of total
gas consumption
supplied by Russia
- 0
- 0.1–24.9
- 25–49.9
- 50–74.9
- 75–99.9
- 100
- Major gas pipeline from Russia
- Gas pipelines
- Gas storage
- Non-EU countries

Russian exports through **Nord Stream and Yamal** 95 million m^3 per day

Russian exports **through Ukraine** 175 million m^3 per day

Gas pipelines from Russia

Figure 8

Extent of Russian taiga

Figure 9

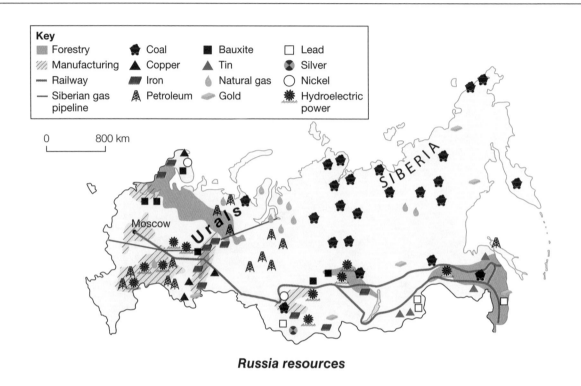

Russia resources

Figure 10

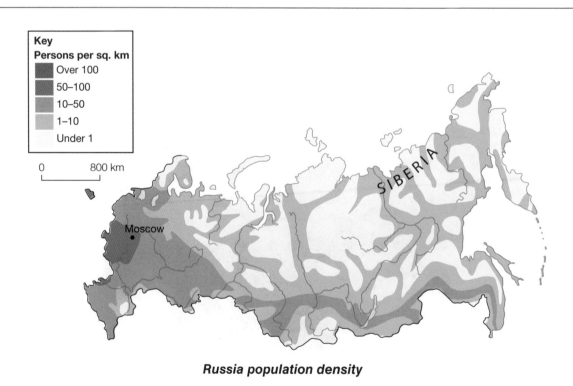

Russia population density

Figure 11

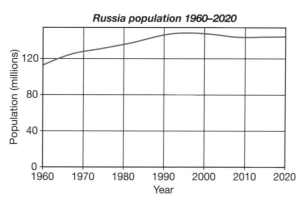

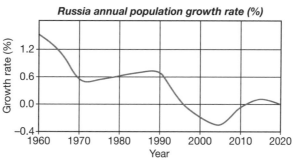

Figure 12

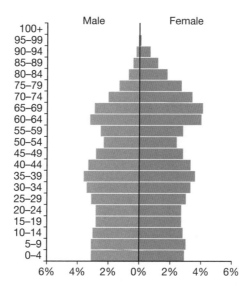

Projected Population Pyramid for Russia in 2050

Figure 13

Many indigenous and local people in Siberia rely heavily on the taiga for timber and the maintenance of their way of life.

Eastern Siberia contains the largest expanse of untouched taiga forest in the world. Russia's largest populations of brown bear, moose, wolf and reindeer live there, as well as rare Siberian tigers and Far Eastern leopards.

Recent estimates of the rates of deforestation in Russia's forests are as high as 20 000 km² annually, comparable to the annual rate of forest clearing in the Brazilian Amazon Basin.

Illegal felling is increasing, and now accounts for up to 70 per cent of the total number cut down. Russia loses approximately US$1 billion per year due to illegal logging and trade which, in turn, restricts money available for sustainable forestry and community development.

Forest fires are a major threat to the region. The average annual forest loss due to fire is approximately 1–3 million hectares. Siberian forests are particularly at risk from fires which are often started illegally. They have increased tenfold in the last 20 years.

Apart from the threat from logging in the taiga, there are also threats from the mining of minerals and fossil fuels and the development of HEP, which can cause oil spills or flooding. There are other environmental issues like acid rain, forest fires and pests/diseases.

Russia has more than one-fifth of the world's forests, which makes it the largest forested country in the world. However, Russia's share of the global trade in forest products is less than four per cent, so there is great potential for expansion.

Thawing permafrost due to forest fires and climate change could increase greenhouse emissions, as a huge amount of carbon stored in Russia's forests is locked in peat that is currently frozen within the permafrost. Thinning of the permafrost can trigger the release of carbon dioxide and methane.

Quotes about Russian taiga forests

Figure 1

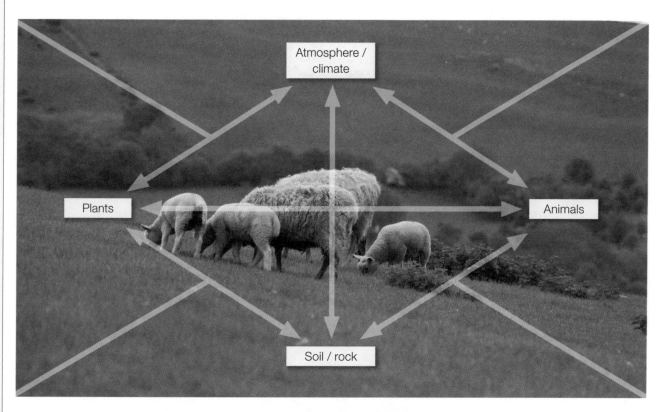

A small-scale ecosystem

Figure 2

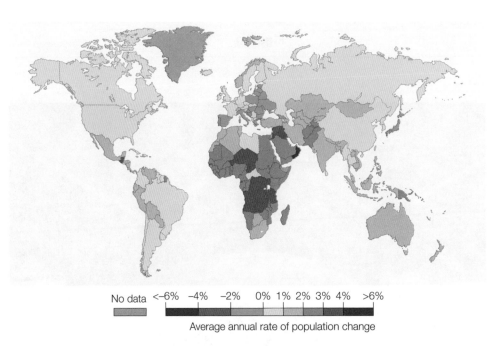

No data   <−6%   −4%   −2%   0% 1% 2% 3% 4%   >6%

Average annual rate of population change

Population growth rate, 2015

Figure 3

Key
- ■ Tundra
- ▨ Coniferous forest
- ▨ Temperate deciduous forest
- ▨ Temperate grassland
- ■ Mediterranean
- □ Desert
- ▨ Tropical rainforest
- ▨ Tropical grassland (savanna)
- □ Other biomes (e.g. polar, ice, mountains)

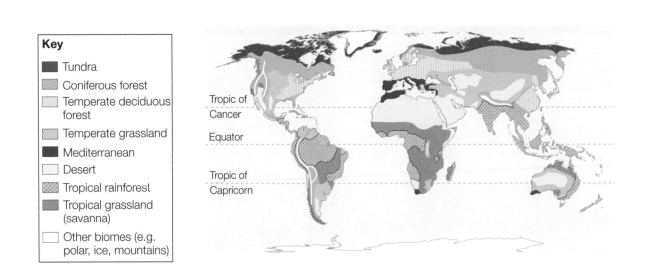

Tropic of Cancer

Equator

Tropic of Capricorn

Global ecosystems

Section B Forests Under Threat

Figure 4

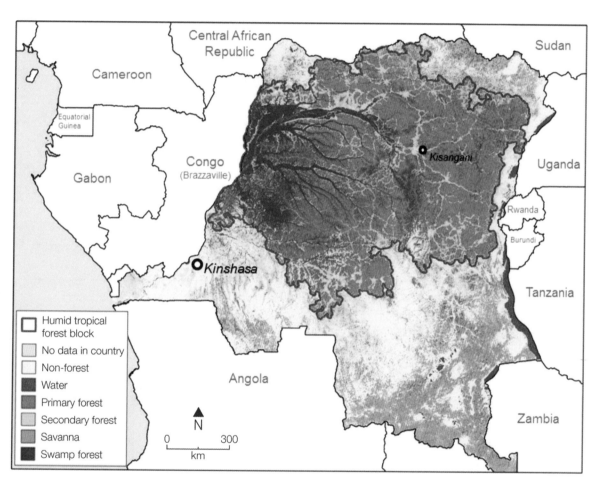

Rainforest cover map of the Democratic Republic of the Congo (DRC)

Figure 5

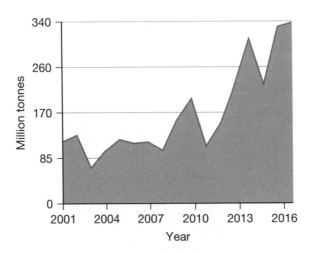

Carbon released into the atmosphere as a result of deforestation in the DRC

Figure 6

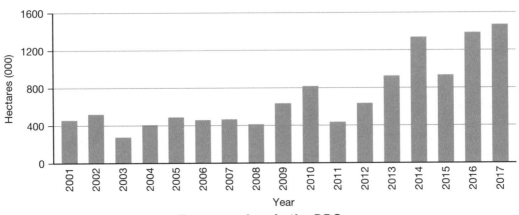

Tree cover loss in the DRC

Figure 7

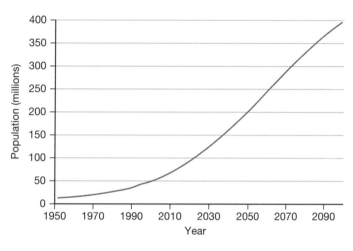

Population growth in the DRC, 1950–2100
The DRC has one of the highest population growth rates in the world

Figure 8

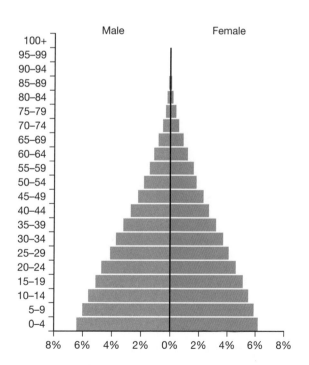

Population Pyramid for the DRC 2050

Figure 9

Birth rate	41/1000
Death rate	10/1000
Total fertility rate	5.7 children/woman
Rate of natural rate	31%

Development indicators for the DRC

Figure 10

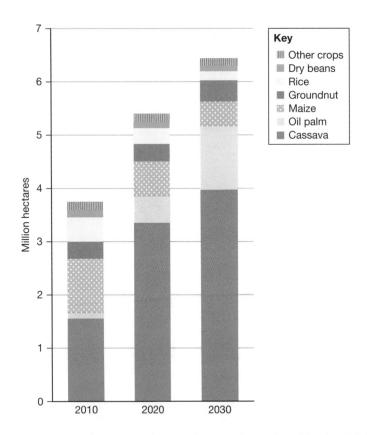

Projected crop production on former forestland in the DRC

Figure 11

| The small populations of indigenous people living in the rainforest rely on the forest for their livelihood. | Patches of rainforest are cleared to plant cassava, corn and yams for themselves and peanuts, rice, coffee beans and oil palms to sell. | They are hunter-gatherers so they hunt animals and they gather foods from the rainforest. |

| Meat is exchanged between farmers for vegetables, grains and other produce. | The women collect caterpillars, grubs and honey to eat along with a variety of plants that they use for food and medicine. | Shelters are made from young trees woven together. |

Ways of life of indigenous people of the rainforest

Figure 12

Firewood is an important source of energy in the DRC

Figure 13

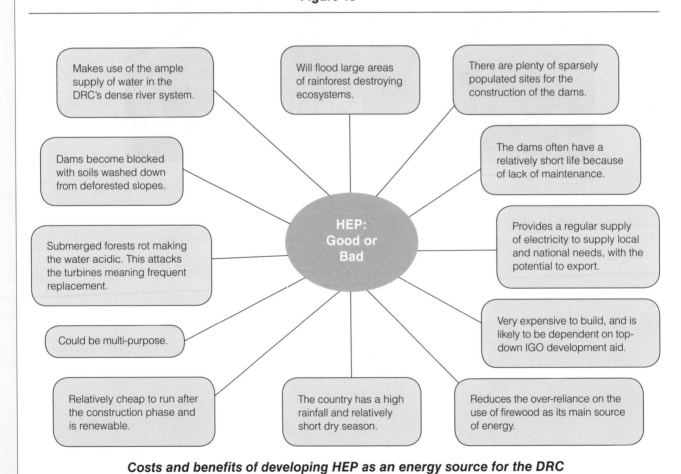

Makes use of the ample supply of water in the DRC's dense river system.

Will flood large areas of rainforest destroying ecosystems.

There are plenty of sparsely populated sites for the construction of the dams.

Dams become blocked with soils washed down from deforested slopes.

The dams often have a relatively short life because of lack of maintenance.

Submerged forests rot making the water acidic. This attacks the turbines meaning frequent replacement.

HEP: Good or Bad

Provides a regular supply of electricity to supply local and national needs, with the potential to export.

Could be multi-purpose.

Very expensive to build, and is likely to be dependent on top-down IGO development aid.

Relatively cheap to run after the construction phase and is renewable.

The country has a high rainfall and relatively short dry season.

Reduces the over-reliance on the use of firewood as its main source of energy.

Costs and benefits of developing HEP as an energy source for the DRC

Figure 14

Inga 1 and 2 dams on the Congo River

Figure 15

Construction of world's largest dam in DR Congo could begin within months

The DRC is currently experiencing an energy crisis because of the lack of proper investment and management in the energy sector. Some 93.6% of the country is highly dependent on wood fuel as main source of energy. This is having severe impacts, such as deforestation and general degradation of the environment.

The largest dam in the world is set to begin construction within months and could be generating electricity in under five years.

The Inga 3 project, costing about $100 billion, could eventually span the Congo River, the world's second largest river by volume. It is expected to have the capability to generate nearly twice as much electricity as the Three Gorges Dam in China.

Critics have said that 60 000 people may have to move, and that fish supplies from the river are likely to be greatly affected. Developing Inga 3 without an environmental impact assessment will violate national law and international guidelines. 'There has been a complete disregard for affected people and the environment. It is shocking that the world's biggest hydropower scheme could go forward without an assessment of its social and environmental impacts.'

Supporters say that Inga 3 is the 'only solution' to the DRC's energy problem and would allow it to export electricity… 'As Congolese we have no choice but to build Inga 3. Today, the price of commodities is falling and we need revenue. If we have a lot of energy to export, like Canada and Saudi Arabia, we won't have a problem'.